KIMCHI

JIHYUN KIM

INTRODUCTION

Welcome to My World

PAGE 6

PART 1

Roots & Rituals

PAGE 14

PART 2

The Craft of Kimchi

PAGE 26

PART 3

The Recipes
PAGE 56

The Classics PAGE 58
A Year of Ferments PAGE 84
Using Fresh Kimchi PAGE 124
Using Mid-fermented Kimchi PAGE 134
Using Well-fermented Kimchi PAGE 146
Blended Kimchi Sauce Collection PAGE 182

Troubleshooting PAGE 184
Glossary PAGE 186
Index PAGE 188

INTRODUCTION

Welcome to My World

My Origins
and Relationship
with Kimchi

A Letter from Kimmy

Dear Reader,

First of all – thank you.

If you're holding this book in your hands, you're already part of the kimchi journey that has brought me so much joy, connection and purpose. Whether you're curious about fermentation, passionate about Korean cuisine or simply looking to bring something bold and beautiful into your kitchen, I'm so happy you're here.

In 2018, I founded Kimchi & Radish from my home kitchen, with just a folding table, twenty jars and a simple goal: to share real, fresh, small-batch kimchi with people who craved something authentic. What followed has been a journey of discovery: of flavours, cultures, community and unexpected kindness.

This cookbook is a way of telling my story. It's filled with recipes I love, traditions I carry and new ideas inspired by life in London. It's a mix of the old and the new, just like me. I hope this book helps you feel more confident in the kitchen, more connected to the food you make and more inspired to explore kimchi in your own way.

Wherever you're starting from, welcome to the table.

With warmth and gratitude,

Kimmy

ABOUT THE AUTHOR

Jihyun Kim, Kimmy to her family and friends, holds Korean nationally accredited cook's certificates in both Korean and Japanese cuisine, earned before relocating to the United Kingdom. In 2006, she completed the Cordon Bleu Certificate at Tante Marie Culinary Academy – an intensive professional chef training programme rooted in classical French culinary technique.

In 2018, Kimmy founded Kimchi & Radish in London, quickly establishing a loyal and growing following. What began as a small venture has since grown into a leading name in authentic, handcrafted Korean fermentation, setting a new standard for kimchi in the UK.

Kimmy's diverse culinary background anchored in East Asian tradition and refined through European technique forms the foundation of her distinctive approach to fermentation. Her work is defined by a balance of technical precision, cultural depth and a deep, seasonal sensibility.

MY KIMCHI JOURNEY

From Seoul to London

I was born in Seoul, in a home that always smelled like something delicious was about to happen. The fridge was never empty, and neither was the table. My earliest memories are filled with warmth, rising steam and the deep red colour of kimchi. I didn't know it then, but everything I needed to learn about care, patience and community was already there in that kitchen.

As a child, kimchi-making days felt like a celebration. My mother, grandmother and aunties gathered around the kitchen table, chatting and laughing, their hands moving instinctively through piles of cabbage and bowls of seasoning. I was too young to join in, but I watched closely. There was no strict measuring – just memory, feeling and years of experience.

When I moved to the UK in my twenties, I brought many things with me: a suitcase full of clothes, a jar of my mum's homemade kimchi wrapped in layers of clingfilm and a quiet longing I couldn't quite name. Life in London was exciting, but different. The food felt unfamiliar, the air smelled different and I missed the taste of home more deeply than I expected.

I began making kimchi again. At first it was just for myself, then for friends. Then I began selling to strangers who became regulars and some even became friends, too. Slowly, it grew into something more.

Kimchi & Radish was born in my London kitchen, one small batch at a time. I started selling at markets, sharing samples and teaching workshops. To my surprise, kimchi resonated with people far beyond the Korean community. It reminded them of pickles their grandmothers made, of foods that took time.

This journey has taught me that kimchi is both deeply personal and quietly universal. It's a way to preserve not just vegetables, but culture, memory and identity. From Seoul to London, my kimchi story has been shaped by distance, discovery and the joy of sharing something that feels like home.

Why I Want You to Make Kimchi at Home

As someone who makes and sells kimchi in glass jars, I've learned how to walk a delicate line between tradition and practicality. Kimchi is alive – it breathes, expands, evolves. The moment it's sealed, the clock starts ticking: gases build, textures shift and flavours deepen. It's this living nature that makes kimchi so special ... and so tricky to jar.

To keep retail kimchi safe and stable, I have to make compromises. I tweak salt levels to control fermentation, I jar just after peak fermentation activity, refrigerate early to slow fermentation down and choose packaging that can handle pressure. Some styles, like young, watery kimchi or delicate leaf wraps, simply don't survive more than a few days in a jar. And while I work hard to make every batch delicious, I'll be honest that shop-bought kimchi can never fully replicate the intimacy of home fermentation.

When you make kimchi yourself, you control everything. The cut of the cabbage, the salt you use, the exact flavour and texture. You get to watch it change – taste it fresh on day one, fizzy by day three, bold and deep by week two. You learn not just how to make kimchi, but how to trust your hands and your senses.

There's a quiet magic in the process: salting vegetables by hand, rinsing them with care, rubbing paste into every leaf. Packing the jar, knowing something inside is beginning to transform. It connects you to your food, to tradition, to curiosity.

That's why I wrote this book. Not so you could follow my recipes exactly, but so you could find your own way. Use the vegetables you love. Choose ingredients you trust. Let your kitchen smell alive. Kimchi is a seasonal ritual, a little science experiment, a comfort food. It's good for your gut, yes, but it's also good for your spirit.

Don't worry if it's not perfect. That's not the point. The point is transformation. Salting. Rinsing. Draining. Mixing. Waiting. Tasting. You'll start to notice how every vegetable ferments differently. How time and temperature shape flavour. You'll begin to imagine new combinations. Maybe kale. Maybe beetroot. Maybe something no one's tried yet.

The flavour you create? You can't buy that. Not in a jar. Not even from me.

So go on and give it a try! If you follow a few guidelines, you'll find your rhythm. Some batches might surprise you. Some might not go to plan. But each one is a step forward and an opportunity to learn, to grow and to reconnect with your hands, your senses and your joy.

My hope is that this book gives you not just the knowledge to begin, but the confidence to keep going, jar after jar.

My Kimchi Philosophies

- I keep the ingredients to a minimum, usually no more than ten. You don't need complexity to achieve depth. What matters is balance, freshness and purpose.

- Kimchi is not a way to revive wilted produce. It has long been used to preserve surplus harvests, but the raw materials still need to be good. Fermentation builds on freshness and magnifies whatever you put in, it cannot restore what has gone bad. That's why I avoid jarred pastes, pre-peeled packs of ginger and garlic (which are often frozen and lack flavour) and powders other than gochugaru.

- There is no substitute for Korean chilli flakes, gochugaru. Only gochugaru provides the proper balance of heat, colour and texture. I cover this in more detail on page 45.

- In Korea, there are dozens of varieties of saeujeot, fermented shrimp of different sizes and levels of saltiness, but in most other parts of the world that range doesn't exist. A clean, well-made, Korean anchovy fish sauce is more than enough, and it is what I use. It is deep, savoury and umami-rich without needing to be mixed with anything else.

For vegan kimchi, I build flavour in a different way, with kelp water and a pinch of salt, or simply by relying on more fresh aromatics, such as daikon, ginger and garlic.

It's a common misconception that kimchi uses or needs a starter culture. This is absolutely not the case. Each batch deserves a fresh beginning and adding leftover juice from an old jar often is not only unnecessary, it can can leave the flavour flat or muddled.

After salting the cabbage, I always rinse and drain. This step is essential: it sets the texture, removes excess salt, and prepares the leaves for clean fermentation. Skipping it, or combining salting and seasoning in one step, leads to limp, overly salty cabbage and one-dimensional flavour.

Finally, kimchi is not fancy or medicinal. It is bold, alive and meant to be delicious. It should crunch, spark with heat and deepen in flavour as it ferments. If it tastes flat, overly sour or like a probiotic tonic, something is wrong. Kimchi is honest food, made with care to nourish both spirit and appetite.

So, What Is Kimchi, Exactly?

Kimchi is Korea's national dish. Kimchi permeates daily life: it is present at every meal, from the most ordinary breakfast of rice and soup to the most elaborate feast prepared for ancestral rites. It lives in our fridges, fills our markets and even colours our language. When Koreans smile for a photo, we say 'kimchi' instead of 'cheese'. It is everywhere, and it is us.

At its most basic, kimchi means vegetables that are salted, seasoned and left to ferment. That definition is technically correct, but it misses the essence. It is a method of preservation born of necessity and perfected over centuries, a balance between salt and water, spice and patience. It is the food that carried us through harsh winters and poverty, and the food that now represents Korea to the world.

Diversity and Adaptation

Today, the most recognisable version is baechu kimchi, made from napa cabbage. Its image – bright red, pungent and stacked in jars – has become synonymous with the word 'kimchi'. Yet this fiery colour is a relatively recent addition. Chilli peppers reached Korea in the late sixteenth century, and over the next four centuries gochugaru gradually became central to kimchi, fully taking hold during the late Joseon dynasty. Before then, kimchi was pale, often seasoned only with salt, garlic and herbs.

Cabbage kimchi as we know it today is just one member of a vast family. There are hundreds of types shaped by season, region and pantry. Some are pale and refreshing, others fiery and dense; some soupy and mild, others aged for months until their flavour turns almost smoky.

Across Korea, geography also shaped flavour. In the colder northern provinces, kimchi tends to be lighter in seasoning and often less spicy, while in the warmer south, kimchi is richer, wetter, and more heavily flavoured with seafood pastes and sauces. Some homes favoured the cooling broth of dongchimi, a watery radish kimchi served cold, while others relied on thick, fiery cabbage kimchi to allow families to store it for months.

Kimchi's versatility and ability to transform itself in so many ways is unique for me – I have yet to encounter this with any other food. You can eat it fresh as a side, stir-fry it with rice or pork belly, fold it into dumplings or whisk it into pancakes. You can sip the brine as a tonic, melt it into cheese toasties, stew it into a bubbling jjigae or braise it into a hearty jjim. Kimchi moves effortlessly between raw and cooked, humble and luxurious, comfort and celebration.

The Craft and the Soul

For me, kimchi has always been storytelling in edible form. When I was younger, my mother would carry containers out to the balcony, peering inside with both duty and tenderness. I remember the taste of her crisp geotjeori in spring and the deep tang of aged kimchi simmered into stews in winter. Later, living in London, I opened my own jars and realised the same transformation had unfolded, thousands of miles away, connecting me to the kitchens I grew up in.

The fizz of a well-fermented kimchi is more than taste; it is a reminder that transformation takes time. You cannot force cabbage into sourness overnight. Nature has its rhythm, and our role is to create the right conditions and wait. Kimchi is patient food, and it teaches patience in return.

This is why kimchi cannot be reduced to a formula like 'vegetables, chilli powder, garlic, ginger, salt at 2–3 percent of vegetable weight, massage until brine forms, and pack into a jar'. That recipe, often seen in general fermentation books, produces fermented vegetables, but it does not capture kimchi. The craft lies in the sequence: salting the vegetables to draw out water and firm their texture, rinsing and draining to balance salinity, preparing a seasoning paste that layers spice with aromatics, coating each piece carefully and packing tightly so fermentation can unfold evenly. Each step requires intention.

Adding Japanese miso, soy sauce, gochujang or the wrong kind of chilli does not make kimchi. Miso has its own proud tradition, but in kimchi it changes the flavour and microbial balance, creating something closer to a miso-pickle than kimchi. Gochujang, already a fermented chilli paste, brings extra sugars and salts that alter proportions and shift the process towards a jang-style pickle rather than kimchi. Soy sauce may appear in some regional or vegan adaptations, but it has never been a central ingredient in traditional kimchi.

Kimchi is a living, lactic acid-driven process that balances salt, spice, umami and time. It is not defined by one shortcut ingredient, nor is it interchangeable with any other fermented paste. To keep kimchi's soul intact, we must let vegetables, salt and microbes work together in their own rhythm. That is what transforms cabbage into something more than itself: crisp, tangy, effervescent and deeply Korean.

PART 1
Roots & Rituals

Understanding
the History, Culture
and Craft of Kimchi

THE BIRTH OF KIMCHI

Humble Beginnings: Chimchae

Long before fiery, red-spice coated napa cabbage, early Koreans preserved vegetables out of necessity. With harsh winters halting agriculture, preserving harvests was vital for survival. Using natural salt and water, they submerged vegetables like radish, turnip and cabbage in clay jars called onggi that they then buried. These jars rested quietly beneath the soil, porous yet protective, fermenting in rhythm with the earth. And in that patience, a deeply Korean philosophy: food as care, process as preservation.

These early fermented vegetables were called chimchae (沈菜), meaning 'submerged vegetables'. They contained no garlic, no seafood and no chilli. The flavours were gentle, sour and slightly effervescent – nurtured by time, not heat. This was the seed of what we now call kimchi. The evolution of the word kimchi traces the evolution of the dish itself; language preserving memory. Early terms like chimchae morphed into dimchae, gimchi and finally kimchi over centuries. The changes reflected shifts in pronunciation, script and society.

Eumsik Dimibang and *Imwon Gyeongjeji*

By the seventeenth century, the practice of kimchi-making was not only widespread but worthy of documentation. The *Eumsik Dimibang* (음식 디미방), Korea's oldest known cookbook written by a woman, Lady Jang Gye-hyang, included instructions for salting cucumbers and flavouring them with ginger. While fermentation had been practised and recorded earlier, this was one of the first surviving domestic texts in Hangul to describe such methods for the Korean household.

By 1827, the encyclopedic *Imwon Gyeongjeji* (임원경제지), a comprehensive record of agriculture, food and daily life compiled by Seo Yu-gu, documented dozens of types of kimchi. Some incorporated wild greens, fruits or seafood. By this time chilli had become widespread, though pale or water-based varieties still existed. The diversity shows that kimchi was already more than one thing, even in those early times.

The Gochugaru Revolution

Chilli pepper (gochu) reached Korea in the late sixteenth century. At first, chilli was valued ornamentally or medicinally. Only later did it find its way into the kitchen and once it did, the change was irreversible.

Over time, as Koreans began drying and grinding chilli into the coarse flakes known as gochugaru, kimchi was transformed. Before chilli, kimchi was typically pale and mild, sometimes seasoned with garlic, ginger or herbs. With gochugaru, it became vibrant, spicy and complex. The seasoning paste that developed combined chilli with garlic, ginger, fermented seafood (jeotgal) and radish, creating layers of flavour and depth.

Chilli also gave kimchi its striking red hue, added pungency and may have influenced microbial balance, though the true preservative remained lactic-acid fermentation.

The adoption of gochugaru stands as one of the defining moments in kimchi's history. It marked the shift from simple, sour ferments to the richly seasoned, red varieties we now associate with Korea today.

A Country of Seasons: Kimchi's Regional and Seasonal Diversity

Korea's sharply distinct seasons and varied geography gave rise to a kaleidoscope of kimchi styles. Mountainous regions, fertile plains and coastal villages all developed unique versions of preserved vegetables, shaped by what grew locally and what the weather allowed.

In spring, households prepared geotjeori – lightly seasoned fresh kimchi eaten unfermented. Summer brought yeolmu kimchi (young radish greens) and refreshing nabak kimchi (water kimchi with sliced radish and cabbage). Autumn, the peak of the harvest, was the time for large-scale kimjang: making vast batches of cabbage kimchi to last through winter, alongside radish kimchi such as kkakdugi. In the icy north, families often made dongchimi, a watery, mild kimchi well-suited to snowy months, and favoured lighter seasonings overall.

Seasoning levels and fermentation times varied by region. Southern provinces relied on more chilli and fermented seafood (jeotgal) to help the kimchi withstand the warmer climate, while northern regions favoured lighter, water-based kimchi with subtler flavours. Coastal towns incorporated oysters, anchovy sauce or fermented shrimp, while in some inland areas, grains or soy-based pastes were occasionally added for depth.

A Living Tradition: The Present and Future of Kimchi

Today, kimchi is both traditional and trendy. You will find it in home kitchens and Michelin-starred dishes. It shows up in grilled cheese, fried rice and tacos. It is featured in scientific journals and cultural essays. And still, it is made by halmonis in countryside kitchens much as it was generations ago.

People are now experimenting with kale kimchi, beetroot kimchi and even Brussels sprout kimchi. Vegan versions, low-sodium varieties and single-jar fermentations are making kimchi more accessible. Technology, too, has played a role. The invention of the kimchi fridge in the late twentieth century allowed urban dwellers to ferment and store kimchi in temperature-controlled conditions.

Yet despite these innovations, the heart of kimchi remains the same: preserve the season, feed the family and pass it on.

KIMCHI & KOREAN CULTURE

A Dish That Holds Tradition

To understand Korean culture is to understand kimchi. It is an anchor and an echo. It connects us to season, to ceremony and to each other.

Kimchi appears at jesa (ancestral rites), weddings, harvest festivals and New Year celebrations. It carries the weight of memory and reverence. But the most powerful expression of tradition is kimjang – the communal making of winter kimchi. Families and neighbours gather, preparing hundreds of cabbages for the cold months. The air fills with spice. Hands work with memory. Meals are shared. Stories are passed.

In that mix of red paste and laughter is something sacred. It's generational wisdom kneaded into leaves. It's ritual and resilience wrapped into napa hearts.

In Korea, there is a word: bap-sang. It refers not just to a meal, but to the setting of rice and side dishes that complete it. And there is no bap-sang without kimchi. In daily life, kimchi is essential: in school lunch trays; in lunchboxes packed with care. A Korean meal without kimchi feels incomplete.

Kimchi in Our Words

We speak in kimchi. Everyday Korean language is seasoned with it. One common proverb says, 'Don't drink the kimchi soup before the meat' (김칫국부터 마시지 마라). It is a gentle warning not to get ahead of yourself, much like the English saying, 'Don't count your chickens before they hatch.'

Another phrase, '파김치 되다', literally 'to become like spring onion kimchi', describes being completely exhausted. Just as spring onions wilt and collapse once salted for kimchi, so, too, does a person after a long, tiring day.

A well-loved proverb reminds us, 'Every household has its own kimchi flavour' (집집마다 김치맛이 다르다). Even when the same ingredients are used, the seasoning, the hand that mixes and the rhythm of fermentation always leave their own unique mark. We use it to remind ourselves that no two people are alike; each carries a distinct character and way of being.

Even affection can be expressed through kimchi. I often say, 'I gave them my kimchi,' to mean I gave someone my effort, sincerity or trust.

Kimchi runs through our literature and imagination. It appears in children's songs and stories, in lines of poetry and even in jokes. That a humble jar of fermented vegetables could carry so much meaning tells you everything about how deeply it runs through Korean life.

Kimjang

In 2013, UNESCO added kimjang to its list of Intangible Cultural Heritage of Humanity. To Koreans, this was both a proud recognition and a gentle reminder of something we have always known: kimjang is not just food preparation, it is a cultural cornerstone and a ritual of cooperation, identity and care.

For me, kimjang has always been more than making kimchi. It is memory, labour, laughter and belonging. It is the sound of chatter in cold air, the ache in your shoulders after salting dozens of cabbages, the smell of garlic rising from a giant basin of seasoning paste and the thrill of that first crisp bite of freshly made kimchi.

What Is Kimjang?

Kimjang (김장) is the act of making kimchi together, in community. It happens in late autumn when napa cabbage is in season and the weather is cool. Traditionally, the results fed families through winter.

But kimjang is more than a culinary event, it's a ritual of preservation, cooperation and cultural memory. Entire communities gather: elders plan the schedule and oversee the seasoning; younger family members lift, stir and stuff; and children run around stealing slices of salted radish, giggling with red-stained fingers.

It begins with the sting of cold water as dozens, sometimes hundreds, of cabbages are washed in large basins. Then comes the brining: salt rubbed meticulously between each leaf. The kitchen fills with the sharp scent of gochugaru, garlic and ginger paste. The noise of slicing, stirring and laughter rises like a chorus.

People talk while they work. They swap gossip, tell stories, argue gently over seasoning. You see who's aged, who's pregnant, who's hurting. And then you feed them. When it's done, there's the quiet pride of stacked jars, lined like soldiers ready for winter. Afterwards, there is always a feast – boiled pork (bossam), rice and the first taste of fresh kimchi.

Kimjang Then and Now: A Living Tradition

In the past, kimjang began with careful planning. Families calculated how many heads of cabbage were needed for the winter, often upwards of fifty or more. The whole process spanned days: harvesting vegetables, drying them in the sun, salting, rinsing, preparing seasoning paste and stuffing each cabbage by hand.

It was physically demanding but that labour brought people together. It wasn't just a task, it was a shared experience – if one household was making kimchi, others pitched in, knowing their turn would come next week.

People gathered with aprons tied, gloves on and sleeves rolled up. The elders passed down knowledge on how to trim the cabbage just right, how salty the paste should taste before fermentation. There were no written recipes, just the rhythm of remembering hands. Once held in the open courtyards of rural villages, kimjang today takes many forms. In modern Korea, the practice has adapted to apartments, urban schedules and convenience, but it hasn't disappeared.

Among young Koreans rediscovering traditional foodways, there is a renewed respect for the practice. Some see it as a form of slow living. Others regard it as cultural resistance to fast-paced, convenience-driven lifestyles.

The scale may be smaller, the containers may be plastic instead of clay, but the meaning remains. Whether it happens in a village courtyard or a London apartment, kimjang is still a living tradition and one that honours the past while feeding the future.

Kimjang in the Diaspora: Korean Kitchens Abroad

Today, kimjang takes place not only in Korea but around the world. Korean families in Canada, Australia, the UK and beyond have brought their traditions with them. In some cases, kimjang is even more sacred overseas as it has become a way to stay connected to home, to roots and to memory.

In London, kimjang might happen in a small kitchen with British-grown napa cabbage, sea salt from Cornwall and daikon from a Chinese market. Daughters video call their Korean mothers for seasoning tips. Neighbours pass jars through fences or over walls. Community groups host kimjang workshops and invite non-Koreans to participate. What matters isn't exact replication but the spirit of preparation, generosity and celebration.

A LANDSCAPE OF FLAVOUR

Each region of Korea, from the volcanic coastline of Jeju to the steep slopes of Gangwon-do, tells a distinct story of place through its kimchi. These stories are shaped by local geography, climate, seasonal harvests and generational customs. To explore the regional styles of kimchi is to trace a map of the Korean peninsula in fermentation, one that speaks of resilience, abundance, survival and celebration.

Where you are in Korea has always shaped what you ferment and how. Coastal towns are rich with anchovy sauce and oysters, while inland farming communities rely more on radishes and freshwater. The long winters of the north demanded slow-fermenting, water-based kimchi. The warm south developed bold, spicy, salty flavours to resist quick souring. In courtly Seoul, kimchi became refined – mild, balanced and beautiful.

As we travel through these regional kimchi traditions, we begin to understand how kimchi connects to everything. What follows is not a definitive list, but forms part of a living archive of Korea's flavour geography.

Jeolla-do Kimchi: Abundant, Umami-rich and Boldly Flavoured

The provinces of Jeollabuk-do and Jeollanam-do, located in Korea's fertile southwest, are known for their culinary depth and diversity. Abundant coastal access and rich agricultural plains define the food culture here. Kimchi from this region is famed for its bold, layered flavours and generous use of seasoning. Its intensity makes it particularly suited for slow-cooked dishes like kimchi jjim and braised meats.

This is a region that embraces depth and complexity. Multiple types of fermented seafood, such as salted shrimp, anchovy extract and even fermented oysters are blended into the seasoning. The result is kimchi that is rich in umami and vibrant in colour, with a distinctive red hue from liberal use of gochugaru. The climate here is mild, with longer growing seasons, allowing for a greater variety of vegetables to be used, from mustard leaves to young radish greens.

Gyeongsang-do Kimchi: Bold, Salty and Full of Heat

Located in Korea's southeast, the Gyeongsang provinces of Gyeongsangbuk-do and Gyeongsangnam-do are shaped by coastal fisheries and hot summers. With heat accelerating fermentation, the people of Gyeongsang-do developed techniques to slow the process, such as using less water and more salt, giving rise to kimchi that is intensely seasoned, highly salted and full of spice.

Anchovy sauce is the star here. It is often used in large quantities to bring briny depth and assertiveness. Other seafood products, like fermented saury or hairtail entrails, lend strong umami tones. The vegetables are often brined for longer and pressed drier, resulting in a chewier texture and less liquid in the jar.

Its robust flavour is perfect for use in stir-fried kimchi, hot stews and bold rice dishes that need a punch of seasoning.

Seoul and Gyeonggi-do Kimchi: Refined, Elegant and Balanced

Seoul, South Korea's capital and home to centuries of royal history, developed a distinctive culinary style marked by restraint and refinement. Surrounded by Gyeonggi-do, a province with both bustling cities and farmlands, the region balances urban elegance with seasonal sensibility. The result is kimchi that is well-balanced, visually appealing and lightly seasoned.

Courtly traditions shaped the flavours here. Rather than overwhelming the palate, Seoul-style kimchi aims for harmony – slightly sweet, moderately salty and never too spicy. The use of fruit, like pear and apple, to sweeten the seasoning paste is common. Fermented seafood is used sparingly, often limited to high-quality saeujeot (salted shrimp) or yellow croaker sauce.

Decorative styles emerged here too: bossam kimchi, where fillings are elegantly wrapped in cabbage leaves; jang kimchi, fermented with soy sauce; and geotjeori, a lightly dressed fresh kimchi for immediate consumption. These are styles that prioritise aesthetics and balance, making them suitable for ceremonial and everyday meals alike.

Gangwon-do Kimchi: Mountain Simplicity, Coastal Salinity

Gangwon-do, with its stark divide between inland mountains and eastern coastline, brings together two contrasting food cultures. The inland areas, including regions like Yeongseo, are known for their harsh winters and limited growing seasons. Kimchi here tends to be simpler, often relying on hardy crops like cabbage and radish, with minimal seasoning and little or no jeotgal.

The mountainous climate meant kimchi has to last through cold months. Clean, fresh-tasting water from mountain springs often features in preparations like dongchimi – a mild, watery radish kimchi that offers hydration and lightness. Seasoning is restrained, focusing on the inherent flavours of the vegetables.

On the coast, Yeongdong residents enjoy more access to seafood. Their kimchi often includes pollack, squid and anchovy. A unique variety here is squid kimchi, where fresh squid is mixed with radish and light chilli seasoning for immediate consumption.

Chungcheong-do Kimchi: Mild, Practical and Rooted in Season

Chungcheong-do sits in Korea's central region, and its culinary approach is often described as modest and restrained. The region's dialect is slow and soft, and the food mirrors this cultural calm. Kimchi here is less aggressively seasoned than in neighbouring provinces. There's less chilli, less salt and often fewer kinds of jeotgal.

The agricultural environment provides a steady yield of seasonal vegetables, which are often used fresh and not overly manipulated. Chungcheong-do kimchi is about allowing the ingredients to speak for themselves. The use of fresh herbs, soybean sprouts, aubergines or courgette reflects a frugal, ingredient-driven tradition, as does baechu gogaengi kimchi, made with the cabbage cores. While the taste might be milder, these kimchi styles develop complexity as they age, making them perfect for slow winter fermentation or for eating with clean-flavoured soups.

Jeju-do Kimchi: Foraged, Briny and Minimalist

Jeju Island, Korea's southernmost province, offers a distinctive approach to kimchi. The island's volcanic soil, strong winds and limited freshwater sources have shaped its culinary history. Napa cabbage does not grow well here, so kimchi is often made with alternative greens: mustard leaves, radish tops or even seaweed.

The island's residents relied on what they could gather or grow locally. As a result, Jeju kimchi uses very little seasoning in terms of chilli, sugar and jeotgal. Instead, local seafood such as anchovy, abalone or mullet provides natural salinity. The result is a light, chewy kimchi that tastes of the sea and preserves the identity of its core ingredients.

Tot kimchi, made with hijiki-like seaweed, is one of Jeju's most iconic varieties. It is chewy, salty and fresh, often eaten with grilled fish or barley rice.

North Korean Kimchi: Cool, Clear and Quietly Complex

Although North Korea remains largely closed, traditional Northern kimchi styles have been preserved through diaspora communities and historical records. Northern regions, including Pyongan-do and Hamgyong-do, have extremely cold winters and shorter growing seasons. These environmental conditions have shaped a kimchi that is less spicy, less salty and more delicately layered.

Instead of gochugaru, Northern kimchi often uses chilli threads or mild flakes. Seasoning is mild, allowing for flavours to deepen over long storage. Fermentation is often topped with saltwater stock to preserve moisture and slow souring. Jeotgal is used sparingly, either light fish sauce or none at all, and sliced pear, pine nuts or jujubes are often added for sweetness.

Water kimchi, or mul kimchi, is particularly associated with the North. It is refreshing, lightly brined and served chilled. These kimchi types are well-suited to be paired with hearty grains like barley, cold noodles or steamed root vegetables.

A Fermented Geography of the Korean Peninsula

What emerges from this tour of Korea's regional kimchi is a map of taste, memory and adaptation. From Jeolla's exuberant seasoning to Jeju's seaweed simplicity, from the fiery resilience of Gyeongsang to the elegant restraint of Seoul, each jar of kimchi is a cultural echo. These are not just differences in flavour but differences in worldview, climate and resources.

To make kimchi is to participate in a conversation with the land. Whether you live by the sea or in the middle of a city, whether you ferment in winter or summer, you are tapping into this ancient and evolving tradition.

As you ferment your own kimchi, consider: What grows near you? What do you have plenty of? What do you wish to preserve?

Let every jar remind you: fermentation begins with where you are.

PART 2

The Craft of Kimchi

From
Ingredients to
Presentation

THE HEART OF FERMENTATION

'Fermentation doesn't just preserve food. It fills it with living activity.'

Fermentation is as old as human civilisation. It is one of humanity's oldest collaborations with nature. Long before refrigerators, preservatives or supermarkets, fermentation was how people kept food safe through lean seasons and harsh winters. Yet fermentation was never just about survival. It transformed food: making it tastier, helping nutrients to become easier to absorb, and, in some cases, even creating new ones.

Fermentation is not unique to Korea, nor to kimchi. Every culture has fermented. But each shaped it differently. Salt and time, or yeast and mould, or bacteria with the right conditions: together they turned milk into yoghurt, grapes into wine, soybeans into doenjang, grains into beer and bread, and cabbage into kimchi. It creates the fizz in champagne, the sourness in yoghurt, the umami in miso, and the airy texture in bread. Most importantly, fermentation brings food to life – especially kimchi!

When done correctly, fermentation creates conditions where friendly microbes thrive, and harmful ones usually can't. This is what makes it a relatively safe and time-tested method of preserving food.

In this chapter, we'll talk about how fermentation works in very simple terms. I'll walk you through the three main types of fermentation found in food:

1. Lactic acid fermentation
2. Yeast fermentation
3. Mould fermentation

Fermentation is something anyone can do at home. You don't need to be a scientist or have a lab. You just need curiosity and some patience

Lactic Acid Fermentation: Kimchi, Yoghurt, Pickles and More

Lactic acid fermentation is the most important type for making kimchi. It happens when certain types of bacteria (called lactic acid bacteria) eat the natural sugars in vegetables, milk or grains. As they eat, they create lactic acid, a natural preservative that gives food its sour, tangy flavour. Lactic acid bacteria thrive best without oxygen, though many can survive in its presence. These bacteria protect the food from mould or spoilage and add natural probiotics that can support gut health. But again: taste comes first. Good lactic acid fermentation makes food crispy, tangy, fizzy and full of life.

Common Examples of Lactic Acid Fermentation:

- Sauerkraut – German-style fermented cabbage
- Pickles – vegetables, such as cucumbers, carrots or beetroots, fermented naturally in saltwater brine (different from quick vinegar pickles)
- Yoghurt – milk fermented by lactic acid bacteria

- Sour cream – cream thickened and soured by lactic acid bacteria
- Buttermilk – cultured milk used in pancakes, baking and marinades
- Curtido – a Salvadoran cabbage slaw, often served with pupusas.

Yeast Fermentation: Bread, Beer, Wine and Korean Rice Drinks

Yeast fermentation is different from lactic acid fermentation. Yeast (microscopic fungi) eats sugars and, instead of making acid, produces two things:

- Carbon dioxide (CO_2) – which makes bread rise and drinks fizzy under certain conditions
- Alcohol – which turns grape juice into wine, or rice into makgeolli.

Yeast can grow in both aerobic (with oxygen) and anaerobic (without oxygen) environments. In the presence of oxygen the yeast respires, producing CO_2 and water, but in the absence of oxygen, they switch to fermentation, producing alcohol and CO_2.

Common Examples of Yeast Fermentation:

- Bread – where the CO_2 causes it to rise
- Beer – made from fermented grains, such as barley
- Wine – made from fermented grape juice
- Makgeolli – Korean fermented rice wine with a milky texture
- Cider – made from fermented apple juice
- Champagne – sparkling wine where a second fermentation in the bottle carbonates the liquid
- Mead – made from fermented honey and water
- Ginger beer – made from fermented ginger, sugar and water
- Palm wine – made from fermented palm sap, common in Africa and Southeast Asia.

Mould Fermentation: Doenjang, Miso, Soy Sauce, Cheese and More

Mould fermentation might sound strange, but it's behind some of the richest, most savoury foods we know. Certain helpful moulds grow on beans, grains or dairy, and break down proteins and starches into smaller pieces.

Mould fermentation is aerobic, meaning it requires oxygen. It's slower than bacterial fermentation and often takes months or years. In Korea, we rely on it to make doenjang, ganjang and gochujang.

Common Examples of Mould Fermentation:

- Doenjang – Korean soybean paste, earthy and rich

- Ganjang – Korean soy sauce, brewed from the liquid of fermented meju
- Gochujang – Korean chilli paste aged for months. Gochujang begins with mould-fermented meju but continues to develop with bacteria and yeasts
- Miso – Japanese fermented soybean paste, ranging from sweet white to deep brown
- Tempeh – Indonesian fermented soybeans bound with mould
- Blue cheese – Cheeses like Roquefort or Stilton, made with *Penicillium roqueforti*
- Brie and Camembert – Soft cheeses with white mould rinds, made with *Penicillium camemberti*
- Douchi – Fermented black soybeans used in sauces.

Foundations of Kimchi

Every jar of kimchi begins with decisions: how you cut your cabbage, how you salt it, how you season it and how long you let it rest. These choices might seem minor, but they define everything from the texture and flavour to the longevity of the jar.

Over decades of practice, I've come to trust a handful of simple rules. They do not guarantee perfection as fermentation is too alive for that, but they will keep you aligned with the rhythms Koreans have followed for centuries.

My Five Principles

Don't shred the cabbage.

Kimchi is meant to crunch. Its texture is not negotiable. Shredded cabbage collapses into limp strings, closer to coleslaw than to kimchi. For baechu kimchi (whole napa cabbage), the leaves should be left intact in halves or quarters. For other kimchis, like mak kimchi, don't cut the cabbage smaller than 2 × 2 cm (¾ × ¾ in) squares. This preserves both the juiciness of the stems and the delicacy of the leaves.

The one exception is mak kimchi, the 'everyday' version. Here, cabbages may be chopped into smaller pieces for convenience. The intent is to make it easy to season, scoop and eat. But even mak kimchi is chunky, never slaw-like. The principle is clear: retain structure.

Use only Korean chilli flakes.

No ingredient is more symbolic of kimchi than gochugaru. These flakes are not just about colour and spice but also are the very fingerprint of Korean fermentation. Their texture is coarse enough to cling to cabbage, fine enough to blend into paste. Their heat is measured: warm, fruity and slow to bloom. Their colour is brilliant scarlet, signalling life.

Substitutions won't produce authentic kimchi. Cayenne burns sharply, without depth. Paprika smoulders dully. Fresh chillies bring heat but no body, often making kimchi watery. Gochugaru is non-negotiable.

Avoid miso, soy sauce and gochujang.

This one surprises many non-Korean readers. Aren't miso and soy sauce fermented? Isn't gochujang Korean? Yes, but they are not kimchi.

Miso is Japanese, soy sauce is pan-Asian, and gochujang is a separate Korean ferment that requires months of ageing. Each is beautiful within its own culinary world. But adding them to kimchi blurs categories that Koreans have always kept distinct.

Use fresh, in-season vegetables.

Kimchi is seasonal by design. Koreans once ate very few fresh vegetables in winter apart from dried greens used in soups, so kimchi preserved autumn cabbages for months. Spring brought quick geotjeori (fresh kimchi), alive with tender greens. Summer meant cucumber kimchi to cool the body in humid heat. Autumn radish was sturdy and crisp, perfect for long keeping. Winter kimchi fermented deeply and slowly, sustaining families through snow. Each kimchi belongs to its season, and when you align with that rhythm, the flavours sing with natural harmony.

Let flavour come before function.

Modern discourse often markets kimchi as a 'superfood', full of probiotics and antioxidants. These benefits are real. But historically, Koreans did not ferment cabbage for their microbiomes – they did it for taste. Kimchi was made to enliven plain rice, balance fatty meats and refresh the body after labour.

Flavour is not secondary to function. When food is vibrant and delicious, health follows.

Fermentation: Sugar or No Sugar?

One of the questions I hear most often is whether to add sugar to kimchi.

Traditionally, sweetness came naturally from the ingredients themselves – crisp radishes, tender cabbages, fresh spring onions or fruits like Asian pears and apples. Refined sugar wasn't a common addition. Instead, vegetables and fruit provided a gentle, layered sweetness that deepened as the kimchi fermented.

Today, some households add a little sugar or syrup. Used sparingly, it can round out flavours. Used more heavily, especially to hurry fermentation, it can push the kimchi towards sharp sourness and soften the crunch more quickly.

In my own UK kitchen, where cabbages are often softer and higher in water, I prefer to wait. I brew kelp water, rich with minerals, to bring a quiet, natural sweetness and balance. It asks for patience, but the reward is flavour with layers rather than a single, one-note tang.

With Sugar	No Sugar
Time to sour: 1–2 days at room temperature	Time to sour: 3–4 days at room temperature
Flavour: Brighter, quicker, sometimes shallow	Flavour: Slower, deeper, more layered
Texture: Softens more quickly	Texture: Crunch lasts longer
Best for: Quick kimchi styles	Best for: Kimchi meant to age

Kimmy's Tips

If you need kimchi in a hurry, a spoonful of sugar can help. But if you can give the cabbage time, it will reward you with its own sweetness and that patience will be worth it.

Storage

Many fermentation books often preach a single rule: keep vegetables submerged under brine. For sauerkraut, this is sound advice. The brine excludes air, which protects the cabbage as it ferments. But kimchi follows a different rhythm. Salted and rinsed vegetables are coated in seasoning paste, packed tightly into a container, and sealed. They are moist but not floating.

Fermentation begins quickly, with lactic acid bacteria multiplying enough to drop the pH to a safe acidic range in 24–48 hours. Garlic, ginger, chilli and fermented seafood add their own antimicrobial protection, while the natural CO_2 bubbles help push oxygen from the jar. In Korea, no weights or airlocks were ever needed – just vegetables, salt and a balance of ingredients.

Traditionally, kimchi was stored in earthenware onggi jars, buried in the ground to stay cool, release gas naturally and protect against pests. Today, most households use airtight plastic or glass containers – stackable, fridge-friendly and odour tight. Either way, the principle is the same: pack the jar 85–90 percent full, leave a little headspace for bubbling and seal. Within a few days, light fizz and tang signal that fermentation is taking place. The jar is then moved to the fridge, where flavour deepens slowly.

The exception is water kimchi, such as dongchimi or nabak kimchi, which is intentionally liquid rich and requires the submersion of vegetables to keep its clarity. But for most kimchi, 'under the brine' can backfire, diluting the seasoning, softening the vegetables and slowing the natural bacterial succession. Once fermentation has begun, exposed edges are safe – the acidity protects them. A harmless white film of Kahm's yeast may form, easily scraped off. If it's fuzzy or coloured, that's mould and the entire batch must be discarded. Scraping is not safe, as mould hyphae can spread invisibly into the brine and vegetables. Extra liquid is normal, released as the vegetables soften.

The rhythm of kimchi storage is simple: salt until pliable, coat with paste, pack firmly, ferment briefly at room temperature then move to cold storage. If it turns too sour, cook with it. If it fizzes too quickly, refrigerate sooner.

Kimchi vs. Sauerkraut

Some mistakenly define kimchi as a kind of 'advanced' sauerkraut. However, this is not accurate. Kimchi is its own universe.

Yes, kimchi and sauerkraut share the same microbial foundation: lactic acid bacteria consume sugars, release lactic acid and preserve vegetables with a tangy brightness. Other than that, however, their paths diverge. Sauerkraut is made by shredding cabbage, mixing it with salt, and pressing until enough liquid is drawn out to submerge the cabbage in its own brine. It then ferments steadily, developing a crisp sourness and a flavour that is direct and uncluttered – what some describe as 'clean'.

Kimchi, by contrast, is salted cabbage or radish that is rinsed and coated in a vibrant seasoning paste of garlic, ginger, spring onions, gochugaru, seafood, fruit and sometimes juk (rice porridge). Where sauerkraut is brine-led and straightforward, kimchi is aromatic, layered with spice, sweetness and savoury depth.

Respecting both ferments means precision: sauerkraut is excellent in brined simplicity, kimchi is excellent in seasoned depth.

FERMENTATION DAY BY DAY

Kimchi is not just food sitting quietly in a jar – it is alive. From the moment salt touches cabbage leaves or radish chunks, a chain of invisible changes begins. Over days and weeks, vegetables that began as crisp and raw turn tangy, gently sparkling, complex and nourishing. This is the work of lactic acid fermentation. Naturally present lactic acid bacteria feed on the vegetable sugars, producing lactic acid that both preserves the kimchi and gives it that clean, addictive flavour Koreans describe as 'sseu-reut-da' – refreshingly savoury and sharp.

The guide below shows how kimchi usually develops stage by stage. Use your senses – sight, smell, taste and touch – to follow along. Trusting this process will make you a more confident kimchi-maker and help you know when your jar is perfect for the dish you want to create.

Kimchi Timeline at a Glance

Day	Stage	What It's Like	Best For
0	Just mixed	Raw, crunchy, like a spicy salad	Eaten fresh with hot rice
1–2	Early ferment	Mildly tangy, bubbles beginning	Rice bowls, wraps, light meals
2–5	Active ferment	Juicy, bright, slightly fizzy	Fresh banchan, salads, grain bowls
5–10	Peak ferment	Tangy, balanced, soft but not mushy	Toasties, pancakes, stews
2–3 weeks	Mid-fermented	Deep sourness, umami-rich, softer leaves	Fried rice, dumplings, pork dishes
Month +	Well-fermented	Very sour, deeply savoury, soft	Kimchi jjigae, braises, porridge

Stage 0: Salting – Preparing the Foundation

First the vegetables must be salted. This step is crucial: salt pulls water out of the cabbage or radish, firming their texture and creating a less hospitable environment for harmful microbes.

What's happening:

- Water is drawn out, concentrating flavours.
- The structure of vegetables becomes flexible but remains crisp.
- The right balance of salt lays the groundwork for safe fermentation.

What you'll notice:

- Vegetables become bendable without snapping.
- A light sheen of moisture forms as water is released.
- If you taste a leaf it should be pleasantly salted, never overly salty.

Stage 1: Early Ferment (Day 1–2)

Once the vegetables are packed tightly into a sealed jar, oxygen is pushed out and the fermentation begins. At this stage, the first wave of microbes, *Leuconostoc mesenteroides*, become active.

What's happening:

- Vegetable sugars begin to break down.
- Small amounts of lactic acid and carbon dioxide are produced.
- The environment slowly becomes more acidic, which protects the ferment from harmful bacteria.

What you'll notice:

- Tiny bubbles rising in the brine.
- A clean, slightly tangy smell (not yet sour).
- The flavour remains fresh and the vegetables are still crunchy.

Stage 2: Active Ferment (Day 2–5)

Fermentation now gains momentum. Bubbles form, brine levels rise and the jar begins to feel alive. The baton passes from *Leuconostoc* to *Lactobacillus plantarum*, which will carry the fermentation forward.

What's happening:

- Lactic acid bacteria populations multiply, outcompeting harmful microbes.
- Carbon dioxide increases, giving a natural fizz.
- Acidity rises, flavours blend and textures soften slightly.

What you'll notice:

- A light 'pop' when you open the jar as gas escapes.
- Tangy aromas mingled with garlic, ginger and chilli.
- Vegetables becoming crunchy-tender rather than raw-crisp.

At this point, the kimchi is bright, energetic and perfect as a side dish (banchan), in grain bowls or tucked into wraps. In warm kitchens, this stage can arrive in just 2 days; in cooler conditions, it might take 4–5.

Stage 3: Peak Ferment (Day 5–10, or 1–2 weeks in the fridge)

This is the stage many people consider 'perfect kimchi'. Flavour, aroma and texture come into balance.

What's happening:

- *Lactobacillus plantarum* dominates, stabilising the ecosystem.

- Lactic acid levels rise enough to preserve the kimchi safely.
- Amino acids begin to release from the vegetables, adding depth.

What you'll notice:

- Sourness is clean but not overwhelming.
- Ingredients taste like one unified dish rather than separate elements.
- The brine looks cloudy and may foam slightly when opened.

This stage is incredibly versatile: kimchi fried rice, kimchi pancakes, grilled cheese toasties and soups all benefit from its tangy, lively flavour.

Stage 4: Well-fermented (2–4+ weeks in the fridge)

Now the flavours deepen further. The cold slows fermentation but does not stop it. The kimchi takes on a more pronounced sourness and richer savoury notes.

What's happening:

- Lactic acid bacteria continue to work slowly.
- Amino acids and glutamates increase, giving umami depth.
- Leaves soften, sometimes becoming translucent.

What you'll notice:

- A stronger sourness, almost wine-like.
- Milky or white sediment in the brine – harmless lactic acid bacteria and spice particles.
- A pleasant effervescence in some jars.

This stage is the cook's treasure: perfect for stews (jjigae), dumplings (mandu), braised pork belly and porridge (juk). When the sourness is too strong to enjoy on its own, don't discard it; aged kimchi is a foundation of Korean comfort food.

Temperature and Fermentation Speed

Because microbes respond to temperature, the pace of fermentation is never fixed.

- 0–2°C (32–36°F) (very cold fridge): Fermentation almost stops.
- 3–5°C (37–41°F) (standard fridge): Very slow, best for keeping kimchi at the flavour you like for longer before sourness increases.
- 15–21°C (59–70°F) (room temperature): Active fermentation.
- 25–30°C (77–86°F) (hot kitchen): Very fast – check daily.

Kimmy's Tips

- In winter, let kimchi sit at room temperature for a day or two before chilling.
- Always pack tightly and leave 2cm (¾in) of headspace for pressure from the gases to build and to allow for a buffer against leakages. Sealed containers should be 'burped' at

least once a day during the first 7 days of active fermentation, to prevent the pressure building too high.
- Use sealed containers to keep oxygen out and flavours in.

Good vs. Bad Signs

Good signs:

- Cloudy, bubbly brine
- Tangy, savoury aroma
- A little fizz or pressure released when opened
- White, milky sediment.

Bad signs:

- Rotten, putrid or sickly sweet smell
- Fuzzy mould on the surface (discard whole jar if extensive)
- No signs of activity after 5 days at room temperature (likely too salty or too cold).

Kimmy's Notes

- **Temperature = speed:** A summer batch may ferment in 2 days; winter batches may take a week.
- **Taste daily:** Starting on day 2, a small bite each day teaches you your personal preference.
- **Headspace matters**: Leave room at the top of your jar or risk overflow.
- **Airtight, not airlocked:** Kimchi doesn't require weights or water seals – just tight packing and a sealed jar.
- **Burping the jar:** When kimchi ferments, it produces natural gases (mainly carbon dioxide). If the jar is sealed tightly, pressure can build up inside – sometimes enough to push liquid out. To prevent this, you can 'burp' the jar by opening the lid very briefly once a day during the first few days of active fermentation, then close it again.
- **The fridge is pause, not stop:** Cold slows fermentation, but the jar is still alive.

Final Thoughts: Flavour in Motion

Do not chase a single 'perfect' point. Instead, learn to recognise and enjoy the flavours you love most, whether it's the brightness of young kimchi or the depth of a month-old jar. Taste often, trust your senses and remember: each jar is alive, carrying both your hands' work and the invisible labour of microbes.

This is the joy of kimchi. It's ever-changing, deeply personal and uniquely yours.

SALT: WHAT IT DOES, WHAT TO USE & HOW TO USE IT

When people think about what gives kimchi its bold flavour, they usually picture red chilli flakes, garlic or ginger. But the real magic starts with something much quieter: salt. Salt's role in kimchi isn't just to season, it's to shape.

- It draws out moisture – Salt pulls water out of the vegetables, helping them soften and creating a natural brine. This brine is what protects the ferment and carries flavour deep into every leaf and cube.
- It controls fermentation – The right amount of salt slows things down, keeping bad bacteria away and giving beneficial bacteria (especially lactic acid bacteria) the right environment to thrive. This is what gives kimchi its tangy, clean flavour.
- It affects texture – Too little salt, and your cabbage may rot. Too much, and it'll turn rubbery. Just enough and it stays crisp, bright and delicious.

Without the right kind and the right amount of salt, your kimchi may not ferment properly: it might spoil early, or end up too soft, too salty or simply flat in flavour. This chapter will explain why salt matters so much, and how to choose the best one.

The Traditional Salt: Korean Solar Salt (Cheonil Yeom, 천일염)

In Korea, the gold standard salt for making kimchi is cheonil yeom, or Korean solar salt.

What to know:

- It's harvested from seawater and dried naturally in the sun and wind.
- It's coarse, slightly damp and full of healthy minerals like magnesium and calcium.
- It tastes soft, not sharp.
- It draws moisture slowly, helping cabbage stay crisp during salting.
- Most importantly, it supports long, even fermentation.

In kimjang, families often use solar salt that they've aged for a year or longer, which mellows it out even more.

Practical and versatile: Kosher Salt

Kosher salt is a popular choice among chefs and home cooks alike, and for good reason. It's widely available, easy to handle and generally free from additives.

What to know:

- It's typically additive-free, or contains only minimal anti-caking agents (always check the label to be sure).

- The flake size is usually close to ideal (not too fine), so as to draw moisture out gently.
- It has a clean, mild saltiness without the sharp bite some salts can have.
- It dissolves easily in water, making it suitable for salt solutions and brines.

Please note that some brands are coarser than others, and saltiness by volume can vary, but If Korean solar salt isn't available, kosher salt is a reliable and convenient alternative.

Alternatives: Sea Salt Flakes

Sea salt flakes are a good option if you want something clean and natural with great flavour. In the UK, Maldon and Cornish sea salt are examples that have a reputation for high quality, a clean taste and artisanal production methods.

What to know:

- Flakes have a light, papery texture that dissolves easily.
- High-quality brands rarely contain additives, but always check the packaging.
- The flavour is pure, clean and well-rounded, with subtle mineral notes.
- You can crush the flakes between your fingers if you want a finer texture.

Quality sea salt flakes are good to use for kimchi. Do note, though, that their flaky shape means a spoonful is much lighter than finer salts, so weigh to avoid mistakes.

Fine Sea Salt

Fine sea salt may look a lot like table salt, but it behaves quite differently.

What to know:

- It's often free from iodine, but may still contain anti-caking agents, so check the packaging.
- The fine grain size will draw out water from the vegetables more quickly than a coarser salt, but not usually as aggressively as table salt.
- It's often used in everyday cooking and can work for kimchi if you measure carefully. Weighing your salt is again the safest approach.

Fine sea salt is a good fall-back if it's pure and additive-free. Just go slowly and use your hands to judge the cabbage texture during salting.

Alternatives: Food-grade Rock Salt

Food-grade rock salt is coarse, chunky and usually free from additives. It's not as common in Western kitchens, but it's used in some traditional fermentation styles.

What to know:

- It's coarse and crystalline, similar to Korean solar salt in texture.
- If it's certified food-grade, it's safe and usable in fermentation.
- It's essential to weigh it as its chunky crystals pack very differently from other salts.

One downside is that it dissolves slowly, which may lead to uneven salting unless you give it time or dissolve it in water first.

If you've sourced true food-grade rock salt, it can work, but do note it's a little less predictable than other options, especially for beginners.

Last Resort: Table Salt

Table salt, the most common in Western kitchens, is usually very fine and frequently contains additives: iodine (for public health reasons), dextrose (to stabilise the iodine) and anti-caking agents (to prevent clumping).

While these additives are not harmful, combined with fine grain size, they can interfere with kimchi fermentation in subtle ways:

- Iodised salt can sometimes give a slightly metallic or bitter aftertaste.
- In larger concentrations, iodine could inhibit growth of the beneficial bacteria needed for fermentation.
- Some anti-caking agents can introduce off-flavours or chemical notes.
- Fine grains draw moisture out very quickly, making cabbage limp before it's fermentation properly begins.

If you only have table salt, check the ingredients on the packaging. If it lists iodine or anti-caking agents, you can still use it, but if you have a choice (and for better results), it's best to look for something else.

Never Use: Non-food-grade Salt

Non-food-grade salt is sold for de-icing roads, filling water softeners, or agricultural use. It should never be ingested.

It often contains:

- Dirt or grit
- Industrial impurities
- Unknown additives.

If your salt isn't clearly labelled as food-grade, it's not safe for consumption or fermentation. Don't use it.

The Different Salts: A Summary

Type of Salt	Texture	Additives?	Good for Kimchi?
Korean solar salt	Coarse, damp	No	Best, if available
Kosher salt	Flaky, medium	None or minimal (check packaging)	Good
Sea salt (flakes)	Flaky, medium	Sometimes (check packaging)	Good
Sea salt (fine)	Fine	Sometimes (check packaging)	Acceptable
Rock salt (food grade)	Coarse, crystalline	No (if certified food grade/pure – check packaging)	Acceptable
Table salt	Very fine	Yes (typically iodine, anti-caking agents)	Avoid – can interfere with fermentation
Non-food-grade salt	Variable	Not food grade – may contain grit or contaminants	Never use

Measuring Salt: Volume Isn't Always Reliable

A tablespoon of fine salt is heavier than a tablespoon of coarse salt, simply because it packs tighter. That means if you swap coarse salt for fine salt using tablespoon measures, you might accidentally oversalt your kimchi. The solution to this is to weigh it.

Using a digital kitchen scale gives you the most accurate results. Most traditional kimchi recipes use 2–3 percent salt by weight, based on the total weight of vegetables. This will work out to between 20–30g (1oz) of salt per kilo of cabbage or radish.

If you don't have a scale, you can approximate by volume, but if using fine salt, you need to reduce the amount used by 20–30 percent compared to solar, kosher or flaky sea salt.

How to Tell If Your Cabbage Is Properly Salted

After salting your cabbage, let it rest for a couple of hours. Then rinse a piece, squeeze it gently, and test:

- The leaf should bend without snapping.
- It should release a little moisture but still have a satisfying crunch.
- It should taste salty, but not too salty.

If it's floppy, mushy or bland, something went wrong:

Problem	What Might've Happened	Possible Solutions for Next Time
Cabbage too soft or slimy	Salted or brined for too long OR salt amount too much	Check salt measurement OR reduce salt amount OR shorten soak time
Right amount of salt and time but cabbage too soft or slimy	Ambient temperature could be too warm	Store somewhere cooler; use more salt; shorten soak time
Cabbage too firm	Not enough salt OR too short a ferment OR too cold	Use more salt OR lengthen soak time OR move to a warmer area
Cabbage smells odd or yeasty	Used iodised or contaminated salt	Use clean salt

Final Thoughts: Salt Isn't Just a Seasoning

Choosing your salt is the first step towards great kimchi. It may seem small, but it makes a huge difference.

Salt shapes the pace of fermentation. It affects how the flavours develop, how your vegetables feel when you bite into them and whether you end up with something truly delicious or a ferment gone wrong.

- So, choose honest salt. You want it clean and kind, without anti-caking agents or added iodine. Whether it's solar, kosher, sea or rock, and fine or coarse – keep it simple.
- Slow down. Taste. Feel. Choose wisely. Because in kimchi-making, salt isn't just seasoning, it's where the story begins.

THE ESSENTIAL ELEMENTS OF KIMCHI

Napa Cabbage

When you see 'Chinese cabbage' in a Western cookbook or supermarket, it usually means a pale, soft, cylindrical cabbage suited to salads or stir-fries. In Korea, though, baechu refers to something much more specific: a cabbage bred and grown with kimchi in mind.

They may look similar, yet when it comes to kimchi, Korean baechu and Western 'Chinese cabbage' are not the same. Their differences affect taste, texture and fermentation.

Outside Asia, you'll find labels like 'napa cabbage' or 'Chinese leaf'. These usually refer to light-green, loosely packed cabbages about 25–35cm (10–14in) long and 1–1.5kg (2lb 3oz–3lb 5oz) in weight. They're soft, easy to handle and ship well.

Baechu, the Korean napa cabbage, is shorter and much denser, often weighing 2.5–3kg (5lb 8oz–6lb 10oz). Its outer leaves are deep green, while the inner layers are filled with thick, sweet stalks. Firm and crunchy, it ferments slowly and evenly. It's these qualities that make it ideal for kimchi.

Baechu vs. Chinese Cabbage

Both types of cabbage are healthy, low in calories, and high in vitamins A, C and K. However, baechu often contains more natural sugar and calcium, which support fermentation and help it stay crunchy.

In Korea, cabbage has long been grown specifically for making kimchi, and farmers historically selected varieties based on how well they worked for kimjang. They bred for qualities like sweetness, aroma and strength – traits that help the cabbage ferment properly and remain crisp even after weeks or months in a jar.

Chinese cabbage, by contrast, wasn't bred with kimchi fermentation in mind, so while it is nutritious, it doesn't always deliver the same flavour or crunch.

Final Thoughts: Cabbage Practicalities

Baechu is still the most prized choice for kimchi in Korea, but it isn't always easy to find. Korean supermarkets sometimes stock it, and specialist growers may produce it from imported seed, but outside Korea you're more likely to come across Western-grown napa cabbage.

Napa of any kind can make excellent kimchi – use what's easily available to you. The texture and flavour may be a little different from traditional baechu, but with good seasoning and proper fermentation, you'll still end up with something delicious, lively and true to the spirit of kimchi.

Mu (Korean Radish)

When many people outside Korea begin making kimchi, they often reach for the radish they recognise most easily: the long white Japanese daikon, or perhaps a bundle of small red salad radishes. But when it comes to fermentation, radishes are not interchangeable. The choice of radish shapes the flavour, crunch, water content and success of your kimchi. Some radishes remain crisp and savoury after weeks of fermentation, others collapse into soggy, watery disappointment.

In this section, we'll look closely at the three main radishes you're likely to encounter: Korean radish (mu), Japanese daikon and the common red radish.

Korean Radish (Mu): The Fermenter's Friend

Korean mu is short, stocky and surprisingly heavy for its size. Its pale green shoulders fade into creamy white flesh, and when you hold one in your hand, it feels dense and solid. Raw, it tastes peppery and slightly sharp, but never harsh. As it ferments, that bite mellows into a subtle sweetness with an earthy undertone.

The density of mu is its greatest strength. It keeps its crunch for weeks, even months, making it ideal for long-term ferments. This resilience is why it is the backbone of so many Korean kimchi varieties. Cubed, it becomes kkakdugi, one of Korea's most beloved side dishes. Cut into batons, it stars in dongchimi, a light, water kimchi served chilled. Thin slices appear in nabak-kimchi, and strips are often tucked into baechu kimchi to add crunch and depth.

Japanese Daikon: A Useful Substitute

Daikon is longer, narrower and more widely available around the world. Its flavour is mild, clean and faintly sweet, making it versatile in many Asian cuisines. But daikon behaves differently under fermentation. With higher water content and a softer texture, it releases liquid quickly, which can thin out kimchi paste and leave vegetables softer than intended.

That doesn't mean daikon is useless in kimchi – it just requires adjustments. If you're making kimchi with daikon:

- Salt more generously to draw out extra water.
- Cut into bigger cubes so the radish keeps some structure.
- Shorten fermentation time, moving it to the fridge after 3–5 days to protect the crunch.

Red Radish: Best for Fresh Salads

The round, bright-skinned red radishes common in Western supermarkets are almost never used in Korean cuisine. They are sharp, peppery and often slightly bitter, with light, spongy flesh. Their water content is even higher than daikon, and they collapse quickly under salt. Their skins bleed into brine, turning it pink or greyish, and within a day or two, the radish softens and can develop unpleasant odours.

For these reasons, red radishes are unsuitable for long-term kimchi.

Why Mu Matters

Texture is at the heart of radish kimchi. The snap of a cube of kkakdugi or the crunch of a slice in dongchimi is part of the pleasure. Mu was developed precisely with this in mind. Its dense flesh absorbs salt evenly, producing a reliable, crisp ferment. In contrast, daikon tends towards softness, while red radish collapses almost instantly.

If you can find Korean radish, always choose it. Look for one that feels heavier than expected, with smooth skin, green shoulders and no cracks or softness. Store unwashed, wrapped in newspaper, in the fridge for 2–3 weeks.

Side-by-side Comparison

Feature	Korean Radish (Mu)	Japanese Daikon	Red Radish
Shape	Short, stout	Long, tapered	Small, round
Flavour	Peppery, earthy, sweetens with age	Mild, clean	Sharp, bitter
Texture	Dense, crisp	Softens quickly	Spongy, watery
Water content	Moderate	High	Very high
Fermentation	Holds shape, deepens flavour	Becomes soft, lighter taste	Collapses, colours brine
Best For	All traditional kimchi	Short-term kimchi substitute	Fresh salad, quick pickle

Gochugaru (Korean Chilli Flakes)

If you're new to making kimchi, one of the first questions that might cross your mind is: 'Can I substitute gochugaru with something else?' Maybe you're eyeing that jar of chilli flakes in your cupboard. Or thinking fresh red chilli might make a fiery, colourful stand-in.

The answer is simple. No, gochugaru cannot be replaced.

There are two main types of gochugaru:

- Coarse (Gulgeun Gochugaru, 굵은 고춧가루): The standard type used for kimchi. Gulgeun means 'coarse', and the flakes are soft, slightly larger than paprika powder, without hard seeds. They give kimchi its vivid colour, allow the seasoning paste to cling evenly to the vegetables and add gentle body to the mixture.
- Fine (Goun Gochugaru, 고운 고춧가루): This is ground finer, like powder. It's often used in sauces or finishing touches, not kimchi. Some cooks blend a little fine gochugaru into kimchi paste for deeper colour, but the backbone is always coarse.

What Is Gochugaru?

Gochugaru (고춧가루) is the Korean word for chilli flakes, made from sun-dried Korean red peppers. They've been cultivated in Korea over centuries to deliver a sweet, warm, fruity heat without the harsh sharpness found in many global varieties. The most prized type is known as taeyangcho (태양초), literally 'sun-dried peppers'.

That slow drying process is key. Unlike machine-dried or roasted chilli powders that can taste bitter or acrid, sun-drying preserves the pepper's natural sugars and essential oils. The result is a flake that is hot but also aromatic, balanced and bright.

Good gochugaru has a soft, clingy texture that forms a paste easily with garlic, ginger and jeotgal. It carries a deep ruby-red colour, never oily or artificial, and when you taste it you'll notice not just heat but a hint of sweetness, a clean bite and even a whisper of smokiness from time in the sun. Korean gochugaru comes in mild, medium and hot. Most recipes use medium, but you can blend with mild for gentler heat. Always use Korean gochugaru for authentic flavour and texture.

Fresh red chillies are common in Korean cooking – eaten raw, stir-fried or pickled – but never used as the primary source of spice in kimchi. They cause three major problems:

1. Extra moisture: Fresh chillies are too watery. They make the seasoning paste runny.
2. Inconsistent heat: Different chilli varieties vary wildly in spice. Gochugaru is consistent.
3. Spoilage risk: Fresh juices interfere with the delicate balance of salt, sugar and acidity that makes kimchi ferment safely.

Over generations, fermentation techniques and pepper cultivation shaped one another. The flake's chemistry is perfectly suited to the job: it balances salt, supports lactic acid bacteria and creates the vivid red-orange bloom that makes kimchi both beautiful and appetising. Its heat is rounded and slow-building, so it complements long fermentation without overwhelming the palate. This is why elders say, 'Gochugaru doesn't just make it spicy – it makes it taste like kimchi.'

I Can't Find Gochugaru, What Should I Do?

The honest answer: **Wait.**

Kimchi is a fermented food; it takes time, and it's worth waiting to do it right.

If you're in the UK, US, Canada or Australia, you can find gochugaru online or in most Korean or Asian supermarkets. Look for bags that say:

- 100% Korean chilli pepper
- No added salt, oil or preservatives
- Product of Korea

Gochugaru contains natural oils that can spoil if left at room temperature. Store it in the fridge or freezer once opened. This keeps the flavour fresh, the colour bright, and prevents the oils from turning rancid. A 500g (1lb 2oz) bag will stay vibrant for months when kept cold.

Garlic, Ginger & Jeotgal

While napa cabbage, radish and other vegetables can provide the structure and crunch of kimchi, it's the flavour of garlic, ginger and jeotgal that breathes life into every batch.

Working in harmony, they build complexity, awaken umami and support the vital fermentation process, transforming salted vegetables into something bold, bright and beautifully Korean.

Garlic

Garlic is absolutely essential to kimchi. Beyond its sharp aroma and pungent bite, garlic brings depth that evolves throughout the fermentation process. The sulphur compounds in garlic break down slowly, creating rich, savoury, almost meaty flavours that give kimchi its signature intensity. Additionally, it carries a natural sweetness that helps to balance out salt and spice. When garlic is chopped, the enzyme alliinase produces allicin, a compound that shapes flavour and helps control unwanted microbes, supporting a clean fermentation environment.

	Korean Garlic	**Western Garlic**
Size and structure	Smaller, denser cloves	Larger, airier cloves
Aroma	Sharper, cleaner, spicier	Milder, sometimes musty
Flavour	Deep, long-lasting umami	Lighter, occasionally bitter

When shopping, look for garlic bulbs that are firm, ivory-white and free from green sprouts or dark patches. These are signs of ageing and bitterness.

Preparation tips:

- Peel completely: Even the thinnest skin can turn bitter when grated.
- Mince or purée: Use a sharp knife or food processor to make a fine paste for even distribution.
- Rest before mixing: Let the grated garlic sit for 5–10 minutes before adding it to the kimchi paste. This activates the enzyme alliinase and enhances flavour and nutritional benefits.

Common mistakes with garlic

- Using pre-chopped garlic: Jarred garlic quickly loses sharpness and aroma because its key flavour compounds dissipate once cut.
- Over-puréeing: If you blend garlic too finely or for too long, it can release harsh flavours. A slightly textured mince gives better results.

Ginger

If kimchi was music, garlic would be akin to the bass notes, with ginger providing a light, zesty and clean treble. It lifts the heaviness of garlic and jeotgal with its bright, slightly citrusy warmth. Ginger's natural zing balances the intensity of the paste and refreshes the palate and also contains powerful antimicrobial compounds, which help keep flavours clean while allowing lactic acid bacteria to thrive.

The freshness of the ginger matters. Look for:

- Smooth, taut skin
- Plump, juicy feel when squeezed
- Bright, spicy aroma
- Avoid shrivelled or woody knobs – these are fibrous and difficult to grate.

Preparation tips:

- Peeling: Use the edge of a spoon to scrape the skin off gently without wasting the flesh.
- Grating: A fine microplane or grater works best. You want the ginger to melt into the seasoning paste, not leave behind stringy bits.
- If you spot a fibrous chunk of ginger while mixing, take it out before bottling. Those woody strands don't break down in fermentation and can ruin the paste's silky texture.

Jeotgal

Jeotgal (젓갈) refers to a range of salted, fermented seafood products used widely in Korean cooking, especially in kimchi. It includes shrimp, anchovies, squid, oysters and more.

While you may not see it in the finished kimchi, its presence is profound. Jeotgal contributes enzymes, amino acids and sometimes microbes, all of which enrich flavour and texture.

Jeotgal is often called 'hidden salt' in Korean kitchens because it dissolves into the paste, contributing a round, savoury salinity without leaving big chunks of seafood behind.

Common Types of Jeotgal Used in Kimchi

Jeotgal	Form	Taste Profile	Best For
Saeujeot	Tiny, salted shrimp	Briny, sweet-savoury	Classic baechu kimchi, radish kimchi
Myeolchi Aekjeot	Fish sauce (anchovy)	Salty, pungent, deeply savoury	Lighter kimchi pastes, 'everyday' baechu kimchi
Kkanari Aekjeot	Fish sauce (anchovy)	Delicate, mildly sweet	Summer kimchi or lighter vegetables
Ojingeo Jeot	Fermented squid	Bold, chewy, intense umami	Regional or spicy kimchi styles
Gul Jeot	Fermented oysters	Mineral-rich, oceanic	Premium or celebratory kimchi batches

So, what does jeotgal bring?

- Umami-rich depth: The proteins in fermented seafood break down into glutamates and amino acids, which amplify savoury taste.
- Fermentation booster: Jeotgal contains live enzymes and friendly bacteria that help kickstart the ferment and enrich the final flavour.
- Textural richness: In some recipes, whole tiny shrimp or squid pieces add chewy surprises and tiny bursts of oceanic flavour in each bite.

What if you don't want to use jeotgal?

While jeotgal is traditional, it's not always essential. I often make kimchi in the UK without any seafood and it's still delicious.

Rather than look for substitutes like miso or soy sauce (which can interfere with fermentation), I simply lean into the power of fresh aromatics.

Try adding an extra tablespoon of garlic and/or ginger – using more of these two ingredients can compensate for the depth, brightness and warmth that jeotgal would bring without changing the integrity of a recipe.

Rice Porridge (Juk)

The Role of Juk

- Binding agent: When sweet rice starch is cooked and gelatinised, it becomes slightly sticky. This binding power is what makes a kimchi paste hold tightly to leaves or radish cubes instead of sliding off. A good paste should feel glossy and cohesive, and juk is one of the easiest ways to achieve that.
- Fermentation support: Juk provides a small amount of starch that can break down into sugars, giving lactic acid bacteria a minor boost – especially useful in cooler conditions where fermentation may start more slowly.
- Balancing flavour: Juk adds a delicate sweetness and smooth mouthfeel, rounding off the sharpness of garlic and ginger, softening chilli heat and giving the paste a more polished finish.
- Texture and moisture control: Juk prevents pastes from looking grainy or drying out. It adds sheen and helps the seasoning coat vegetables evenly from the very beginning of fermentation.

Kelp Water Alternative

In my London kitchen, I rarely use juk. Instead, I prepare a kelp infusion for depth and balance.

The infusion brings natural umami and minerals without starch, which I find suits UK-grown cabbage and radish. This method feels lighter, seasonal and true to the spirit of Korean kimchi, while also adapting gracefully to my own environment.

Kelp Water
(Vegan Alternative to Fish Sauce or Juk)

20g (¾oz) dried kelp (dashima), for a fish sauce substitute
30g (1oz) dried kelp (dashima), for a juk substitute
500ml (17½fl oz) cold water

~~~~

1. Wipe the surface of the kelp with a clean, dry cloth (do not rinse under water).

2. Place the kelp in a saucepan with the water.

3. Bring the water slowly to a gentle simmer. Just before it boils, remove the kelp.

4. For the light version: stop here, cool and store.

5. For the concentrated version: continue simmering the liquid for 5–7 minutes to reduce slightly before cooling.

6. Storage: Keeps for 3–4 days in the fridge in a sealed jar.

Freeze in small portions (ice-cube trays or small containers) for 2–3 months. Thaw before use.

~~~~

Kimmy's Tips

You may notice a fine white powder on dried kelp. Don't worry, it isn't dirt, but a natural layer of glutamic acid crystals, which give kelp its deep savoury flavour. If you rinse it under the tap, you'll wash away the natural umami. Instead, simply wipe the surface gently with a clean, dry cloth to remove any grit while keeping the flavour intact.

~~~~

Water

It may seem a small difference, but if you can use filtered water to make your kimchi, I would recommend it. Where I live, in London, is a very hard water area and I can tell the difference both in the behaviour of the fermentation and in the taste of the end product. They may be slight, and even inperceptible to some, but it is there. Tap water is fine to use, but filtered water is better.

PREPARING, SALTING & RINSING

Before You Start

Kimchi making doesn't need a clinically sterilised environment but basic cleanliness is a must – always wash hands, your kitchen utensils, chopping boards and jars/containers with warm, soapy water, followed by a rinse, to remove unwanted microbes.

Preparing the Cabbage

Traditionally, napa cabbages were halved or quartered, their cores left intact. This structure keeps the leaves layered while making them easier to handle. A clean cut, followed by a gentle hand-tear at the base, ensures the leaves stay connected.

Smaller cabbages or quick styles like mak kimchi are cut into chunks. But the principle is universal: every fold in the cabbage leaf must be accessible to salt.

Inspect the leaves. Remove damaged outer layers. Trim the base just enough to tidy it, but never so much that the cabbage falls apart.

Salting: Where Kimchi Begins

After preparing the cabbage, it is salted, rinsed, drained then mixed with seasoning. Korean practice uses both dry-salting between leaves and brine-soaking. Gently pull open each leaf and sprinkle coarse salt – especially on the thick ribs – or submerge the cabbage in 5–8 percent brine (50–80g salt per litre of water or 2–3oz salt per 2 pints). Many homes use a hybrid: salt the ribs, then brine.

Stack the cabbages in large tubs. For brining, keep halves submerged with a plate or shallow bowl for light weight; with dry-salting, weights are usually unnecessary. Let the salt work for 4–8 hours for halves/quarters (very large heads may need up to 10–12 hours). For chopped napa, 30–60 minutes is typically enough.

As osmosis draws water out, liquid pools at the bottom of the container and the leaves become pliable. This is the quiet beginning of kimchi: not yet spiced, not yet tangy, but already changed.

Rinsing: Restoring Balance

After salting comes rinsing. The aim is not to strip salt away completely but to restore harmony. Too much salt slows and skews fermentation; too little invites spoilage.

Rinse the cabbage two to three times in cool running water with quick passes, just enough to remove surface crystals and brine. Avoid long soaks. After rinsing, gently shake water from between the leaves and set halves/quarters cut side down in a colander or on a rack to drain. A short rest lets excess water drip away – vital, because soggy leaves will dilute the seasoning paste. Drain for 20–40 minutes (up to 1 hour for large heads). Never wring pogi (whole/quartered napa), as it damages the leaves and ruins texture; for mak kimchi (chopped), a gentle squeeze is fine.

Now the cabbage is supple, clean and lightly salted. Taste a rib: it should be pleasantly salty, not harsh. The stage is set for garlic, ginger, gochugaru and jeotgal to build flavour.

Salting Day in Memory

> In Korea, salting was never just technical. It was communal. Families and neighbours gathered, children splashed in water tubs, conversations flowed as steadily as brine. The women of the household bent over cabbages with quiet concentration, salting each rib with care, while men carried jars or fetched water.
>
> Salting day was work, but it was also laughter, gossip and kinship.
>
> Today, even in a quiet London kitchen, I feel this memory when I salt cabbage. Each sprinkle of salt echoes a lineage of hands. Kimchi begins not only with flavour but with belonging.

RECOMMENDED TOOLS & FERMENTATION VESSELS

When people ask me what they need to start making kimchi, they often imagine a long shopping list of specialist gadgets. The truth is simpler: good kimchi doesn't require a high-tech kitchen, but it does benefit from a few faithful tools and the right vessels to let it breathe and transform. These are the companions I keep close at hand.

Frequently Used

Large mixing bowl
Wide enough to salt whole cabbage leaves or toss a mountain of radish cubes. Stainless steel or food-grade plastic works best, as kimchi paste can stain wood.

Sharp knife and cutting board
A heavy chef's knife for splitting napa cabbages cleanly, and a smaller utility knife for trimming roots and scoring radishes. A dedicated board for vegetables is ideal, since garlic and chilli flavours can linger in wood.

Colander or strainer basket
To rinse salted vegetables thoroughly. A large colander that fits over the sink lets you drain several cabbages at once.

Measuring scales and spoons
Fermentation depends on balance. Salt especially requires accuracy, so a small kitchen scale is more reliable than handfuls or guesses.

Food-safe gloves (optional, but helpful)
In Korea, kimchi paste is mixed with bare hands and spread leaf by leaf. If chilli burns or garlic stings, thin kitchen gloves can protect while still letting you massage the paste through.

Jars and containers
The final home for your kimchi. They should close tightly enough to control odours and liquid, but not so tightly that gas cannot escape. Glass jars are practical and let you watch colour changes; Korean kimchi containers with snap locks are designed for fridge storage.

Glass jars (Kilner, Mason or Weck jars)
The most accessible option for home cooks outside Korea. Glass doesn't absorb smells, it's easy to sterilise, and it lets you see the bubbles of fermentation. Choose wide-mouth jars for easier packing and cleaning.

Plastic kimchi containers
In modern Korean homes, these are ubiquitous. Designed with snap locks and tight seals, they control odours in the fridge and withstand long fermentations.

Helpful Extras

Fermentation weights
More common in Western fermentation. For kimchi, I rarely use them, since the seasoning paste keeps vegetables coated. But for water kimchi (dongchimi or nabak-kimchi), a small weight can help keep radishes submerged.

Funnels and ladles
For transferring kimchi paste and brine neatly into jars. A wide-mouth funnel saves mess when working with liquids.

Tongs or chopsticks
To retrieve kimchi without contaminating the whole jar. Wooden chopsticks are traditional; stainless-steel tongs are practical.

Kimmy's Notes

- **Don't overcomplicate it:** If all you have is a sharp knife, a big bowl and a jar, you already have enough to make kimchi.
- **Choose size wisely:** A 1 litre (1¾ pint) jar fits about half a medium napa cabbage. For a whole cabbage, 2–3 litre (3½–5¼ pint) containers are more realistic.
- **Think about temperature:** Traditional onggi jars, once buried outdoors, allow gentle air exchange. Modern airtight jars or plastic kimchi tubs suit indoor fridges, and each vessel shapes the rhythm of fermentation s lightly differently.
- You'll find downloadable testing notes on my website: https://kimchiradish.com/kimchibook which you can use to record your ferments, your flavours and your findings. Perfect for beginners learning to trust the process.

HOW TO SERVE KIMCHI

In Korea, kimchi is never an afterthought. Whether it's for a simple Tuesday dinner or a big family feast, the way you serve kimchi shapes how it's enjoyed.

Here's how I serve kimchi so it gets the moment it deserves and how you can do the same, wherever you are.

1. Temperature Matters

- Cool, not icy: Straight from the fridge, flavours can be tight. Let the kimchi rest for 10–15 minutes for the aromas to open.
- Summer: Keep young, crisp kimchi chilled.
- Winter: Bring aged kimchi closer to room temperature, or let it warm gently in stews, pancakes or stir-fries to draw out depth.

2. Choosing the Right Dish

- Everyday meals: Small ceramic or stainless banchan plate.
- Gatherings: Porcelain or lacquer platter, slices arranged in curves or layers to show off colour.
- Rustic tables: Earthenware bowl, echoing the onggi jars of tradition.

Avoid unlined wooden bowls – chilli paste will stain them permanently.

3. Cutting and Arranging

- Whole-leaf (pogi-style): Bring the whole cabbage and slice crossways at the table for a dramatic moment.
- Bite-size chunks: 2–3cm (1in) everyday pieces, easy to pick up.
- Layered slices: Ideal for baek kimchi or stuffed cucumber kimchi – fan them out to show the filling.
- Presentation: Let the vivid red seasoning face outward, with green and white peeking through. For water kimchi, use a clear glass bowl so the brine itself is part of the beauty.

4. Pairing with the Meal

Kimchi balances and elevates the rest of the table:

- With rice: Steamed rice + tangy kimchi = perfect simplicity.
- With soups and stews: Cuts through rich broths like galbitang or soondubu.
- With grilled meats: Aged kimchi refreshes the palate between fatty bites of pork belly or beef galbi.
- With noodles: Young kimchi adds crunch and brightness to bibim guksu or naengmyeon.
- Variety: Offer two or three kinds together – mild baek kimchi beside fiery pogi, crunchy radish alongside soft, aged cabbage.

5. Celebrating Seasonal Kimchi

Match your table to the season:

- Spring: Fresh geotjeori with grilled fish or spring greens.
- Summer: Cucumber kimchi in small bowls, with chilled brine for sipping.
- Autumn: Perilla leaf or pumpkin kimchi with mushroom rice.
- Winter: Deep, aged kimchi with hearty braises or slow-cooked stews.

6. Garnishing and Final Touches

Small touches make a big difference:

- Toasted sesame seeds for nutty aroma.
- A drizzle of perilla oil for earthiness.
- Fresh spring onion slices for brightness.
- Pine nuts or jujube slices for baek kimchi elegance.
- Keep it simple – garnishes should lift the flavour, not smother it.

8. Keeping It Fresh During the Meal

For long meals, keep the extra kimchi in the fridge until it's needed. Kimchi left out too long in a warm room softens quickly and the flavour can turn sharper than you want. For water kimchi, keep the brine ice-cold until serving for maximum refreshment.

9. The Spirit of Serving Kimchi

Serving kimchi well isn't about fuss – it's about respect. Each batch took time, care and tradition. Plating it thoughtfully tells your guests it's not just a condiment; it's part of the story.

When I put kimchi on the table, I'm sharing more than a side dish. I'm sharing something alive – a taste that links my Seoul kitchen memories to the present moment, wherever I am.

PART 3
The Recipes

Classic Styles and
Seasonal Delights

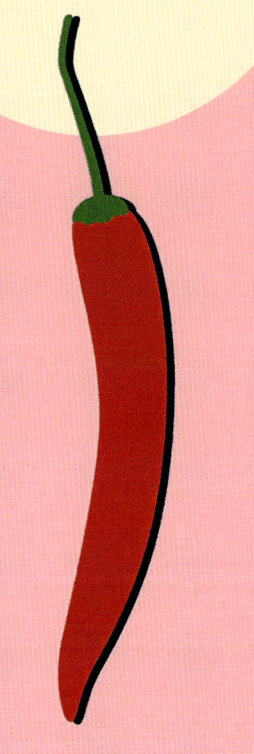

THE CLASSICS

When most people think of kimchi, they picture a jar of fiery red napa cabbage: crunchy, juicy, alive with spice. But to Koreans, 'classic kimchi' means far more than a single style. It is a family of recipes shaped by centuries of survival, adaptation and celebration, carrying the Korean table through every season and generation.

These classics form the foundation of Korean flavour identity. Each has its place: fiery, refreshing, mild or thirst quenching. A typical meal might include three or four together, balancing the table and completing the meal.

What makes them classics is not only age, but resilience. These recipes have survived war, poverty, industrial growth and globalisation. Even today, when factory jars fill supermarket shelves, the classics remain alive in homes, still made by hand with the same gestures: salting cabbage, grinding garlic, stirring gochugaru into paste. They endure as keepers of memory, carrying with them love, labour and continuity.

Pogi Kimchi
포기김치

Prep: 2 hours
Brining/draining: 3 hours 30 minutes–4 hours
Fermenting: 24–36 hours at room temperature before refrigeration
Makes: 1 litre (1¾ pint) jar or container

2 medium napa cabbages (about 2kg/4lb 6oz total), trimmed
160g (5⅔oz) coarse salt, divided:
  100g (3½oz) for a brine
  60g (2oz) sprinkled directly between leaves (salt can be adjusted slightly depending on cabbage density and your taste)
1.5 litres (2½ pints) cold water
1kg (2lb 3oz) Korean radish (mu) or firm daikon, julienned
100g (3½oz) spring onions, cut into 3–5cm (1–2in) lengths

FOR THE SEASONING PASTE

150–250g (5¼–8¾oz) gochugaru, to taste (150g/5¼oz = mild; 200g/7oz = classic; 250g/8¾oz = bold heat and colour)
2 tbsp anchovy fish sauce, or 2 tbsp kelp water with ½ tsp salt
100g (3½oz) garlic, grated
100g (3½oz) ginger, grated
100g (3½oz) pear or apple, grated
150ml (5¼fl oz) filtered water or pear juice (to loosen paste)

Pogi kimchi is the most iconic style of kimchi, made by salting whole napa cabbages and stuffing them with a rich mixture of julienned radish, garlic, spring onions, gochugaru and jeotgal. It's deeply fermented and rich in flavour, often enjoyed young and fresh, but also aged for weeks or months for deeper flavour.

Compared with mak kimchi (the everyday chopped version) on page 62, pogi kimchi holds its shape longer, tastes more composed and ages beautifully: clean and bright when young, savoury and complex as weeks pass.

The word pogi (포기) is a Korean counting unit for whole heads of leafy veg; it signals that the structure is left intact.

1. Prepare cabbage: Lay the cabbage on its side, with the root end closest to your knife hand. Hold the cabbage steady with your other hand. Cut a shallow cross about 5–7cm (2–3in) deep into the thick white base. Then turn the cabbage so the cut faces up, slip your thumbs into the cut, and gently pull the cabbage apart along its natural leaf lines into halves, and then into quarters.

2. Brine: In a large bowl or pot, dissolve 100g (3½oz) salt in the cold water. Dunk each quarter briefly so the brine slips between leaves, then shake off excess. With the remaining 60g (2oz) salt, sprinkle directly between the thicker inner leaves. Return the quarters to the brine, weigh down with some small plates or shallow bowls and leave to soak at cool room temperature for 3 hours, turning halfway.

3. Rinse and drain: Rinse each quarter two to three times under cold running water. Place cut-side down in a colander and drain for 30–60 minutes. Do not squeeze.

4. Make seasoning paste: In a large bowl, combine the gochugaru, fish sauce (or kelp water), garlic, ginger and grated pear or apple. Always include the juice released by the fruit. This is so the paste stays balanced. Add just enough additional water or pear juice until the mixture is glossy and spreadable, but not runny. Let it rest for 5 minutes so the chilli flakes can fully hydrate.

5. Mix filling: Add the julienned radish and spring onions to the paste, tossing until evenly coated. Taste

– it should be slightly saltier than desired in the final kimchi, as the cabbage will dilute it.

6. Stuff cabbage: Wearing gloves, lift each leaf and spread a thin, even layer of filling underneath, from outer leaves inward. Fold the outer leaf over each quarter to wrap neatly.

7. Pack container: Place the quarters snugly into your clean container, cut side up. Press down firmly to remove air pockets; natural brine should rise to cover the kimchi. Leave 2cm (¾in) of headspace, wipe the rim and seal.

8. Ferment: Store at 18–22°C (65–70°F) for 24–36 hours. Check daily for bubbles, rising brine and a light tang. Burp the container daily for the first 7 days, and press down if gaps appear.

9. Store: Once lightly sour, transfer to the fridge to slow fermentation.

Maturity Guide

Day	Texture and Taste	Best For
3–5	Fresh and mild Texture: Crisp, juicy leaves with a light snap Taste: Gentle spice and saltiness	Eating raw as banchan or with plain rice
1–2 weeks	Tangy, deeper flavour and balanced Texture: Softer leaves, still holding shape with a little crunch Taste: Lively acidity, deeper savoury notes	Noodles, grilled meats, tofu
3–5 weeks	Robust and complex Texture: Tender, pliable with a slight chew Taste: Bold sourness, rich umami depth	Stews, pancakes, fried rice

Kimmy's Notes

- **Pear:** Grated pear adds natural sweetness and enzymes that soften texture. Always include its juice.
- **To make it vegan:** Replace fish sauce with kelp water and a pinch of salt. Add extra garlic and ginger for depth.
- **Container:** Don't overfill; gas needs space. Wipe rims before sealing.
- **Taste checks:** Sample on day 2, day 7 and day 21 to learn your kitchen's rhythm.

Mak Kimchi
막김치

Prep: 45 minutes
Brining/draining: 1–1½ hours
Fermenting: 1–3 days at room temperature before refrigeration
Makes: 2–3 litre (3½–5¼ pint) jar or container

1 large napa cabbage (about 1kg/2lb 3oz), trimmed
70g (2½oz) coarse sea salt
500ml (17½fl oz) filtered water
500g (1lb 2oz) daikon, julienned
50g (1¾oz) spring onion, cut into 3–4cm (1–1½in) angled lengths

FOR THE SEASONING PASTE

70g (2½oz) gochugaru
3 tbsp anchovy fish sauce, or 3 tbsp kelp water with ½ tsp salt
50g (1¾oz) garlic, grated
50g (1¾oz) ginger, grated
50g (1¾oz) pear or apple, grated
50ml (1¾fl oz) filtered water

If there's one kind of kimchi I think every home cook should try first, it's mak kimchi. In Korean, the word mak means 'roughly, freely or without strict formality'.

It is a simple cabbage-based cut kimchi. A practical, chopped version of the pogi kimchi on page 59, and is often made in smaller batches. It's fast to prepare and just as flavourful, with all the same seasoning, just less ceremony. It's the kind you make when life is busy, but still want something real, bright and alive on your plate. It's what I grew up eating between big kimjang batches, and what I still reach for on most ordinary days.

---

1. Prepare cabbage: Slice cabbage lengthways into quarters, then cut into 3–5cm (1–2in) squares. Rinse once under cold water and drain briefly.

2. Brine: Place the chopped cabbage in a large bowl. Sprinkle salt as you go, mixing gently. Add the water to help the salt dissolve – the cabbage should be damp, not fully submerged. Rest for 60–90 minutes at room temperature, mixing every 30 minutes. When the leaves bend without snapping, they're ready.

3. Make seasoning paste: Combine gochugaru, fish sauce (or kelp water), garlic, ginger, and grated pear or apple with 50ml (1¾fl oz) water to form a paste. Set aside.

4. Rinse and drain: Drain the cabbage in a colander, rinse two or three times under cold water, then drain thoroughly until no longer dripping.

5. Combine: In the same large bowl, mix the cabbage, daikon and spring onion with the paste. Massage gently with your hands until evenly coated. A little juice should collect at the bottom. Taste it: it should be bold, salty, spicy and slightly sweet – flavours that mellow as it ferments.

6. Pack container: Transfer to a clean airtight container, pressing down to remove air pockets. Leave 2cm (¾in) of headspace, wipe the rim and seal.

7. Ferment: Leave at 18–22°C (65–70°F) for 1–3 days. In cooler kitchens (cooler than 18°C/65°F), it may take a little longer for tanginess to develop. Burp the container daily to release gas. Press down if gaps

form. Taste daily – it should turn tangy, savoury and lightly fizzy.

8. Store: Once bubbling and lightly sour, refrigerate to slow fermentation and preserve crunch.

Maturity Guide

Day	Texture and Taste	Best For
1–2	Crunchy, spicy, fresh	Eating raw as banchan
3–7	Fizzy, bright, aromatic	Bibimbap, noodles
8–21	Tangy, softening	Stews, pancakes
22+	Deeply sour, soft	Broth base, fried rice

Kimmy's Notes

- **Experiment:** Mak kimchi is flexible. You can scale it up or down, adjust the seasoning to taste and experiment with aromatics like chives, wild garlic or other pungents.
- **To make it vegan:** Replace fish sauce with kelp water and a pinch of salt. Add extra garlic and ginger for depth.
- **Ageing:** It's delicious when young and tangy at 1-2 weeks and deeply complex when aged for a month or more.

Pa Kimchi
파김치

Prep: 2 hours
Brining: 20-30 minutes
Fermenting: 24-36 hours at room temperature before refrigeration
Makes: 1 litre (1¾ pint) container

500g (1lb 2oz) Korean jjokpa, or thin spring onions (halve thicker ones)
500ml (17½fl oz) cold water
35g (1¼oz) coarse sea salt

FOR THE SEASONING PASTE

50-75g (2-2½oz) gochugaru
2 tbsp anchovy fish sauce, or 2 tbsp kelp water with ½ tsp salt
30g (1oz) garlic, grated
30g (1oz) ginger, grated
50g (1¾oz) pear or apple, grated
3 tbsp kelp water or filtered water

Kimmy's Notes

- **Onions:** Korean jjokpa are slim and firm. Halve thicker Western spring onions lengthways for better seasoning penetration.
- **Fermentation speed:** Thin onions sour quickly - taste daily and refrigerate once tangy.
- **To make it vegan:** Replace fish sauce with kelp water and a pinch of salt. Add extra garlic and ginger for depth.
- **Storage:** Keep bundles pressed under leftover paste to prevent drying.

Pa kimchi, or spring onion kimchi, is one of the most pungent and powerful kimchi styles. Made with jjokpa (long, slender Korean spring onions) it delivers an aromatic punch that softens only slightly with fermentation. Freshly made, it tastes grassy, fiery and sharp, but after a few days, its bite mellows into a rounded savoury depth.

Unlike cabbage kimchi, pa kimchi is less about crunch and more about chew and aroma, each onion coated in a thick paste from stem to tip. It is a classic partner to samgyeopsal (pork belly barbecue) and hearty soups as its sharpness cuts through fat and broth. Pa kimchi is a reminder that kimchi is far more than cabbage - it captures the essence of every seasonal crop.

1. Prepare onions: Trim roots and any wilted greens, keeping onions whole. Rinse thoroughly. Soak in the cold water mixed with the salt for 20-30 minutes, then drain well.

2. Make paste: In a bowl, combine the gochugaru, fish sauce (or kelp water), garlic, ginger, grated pear or apple and water. Mix into a thick paste and leave to rest for 5 minutes.

3. Coat onions: Wearing gloves, spread paste along each onion from white stem to green tips. Gather into small bundles of four to five onions and layer in a container.

4. Pack container: Press bundles gently into the container, spreading any leftover paste over the top. Leaving 2cm (¾in) of headspace, wipe the rim and seal.

5. Ferment: Leave at 18-20°C (65-68°F) for 24-36 hours, until light bubbling and a tangy aroma develop. Burp the container daily for the first 7 days. Transfer to the fridge once pleasantly sour. It is best eaten between days 5-14.

Serving Suggestions

- Cut bundles into 5-6 cm (2in) lengths before serving, or snip with kitchen scissors at the table for an authentic Korean touch.
- Serve with pork belly barbecue, beef short rib soup (galbitang) or plain rice.
- Try as a topping for cold noodles or folded into an omelette.

Buchu Kimchi
부추김치

Prep: 15 minutes
Brining: None
Fermenting: 2–3 hours at room temperature for wilting, then 2–3 days in the fridge for best flavour
Makes: 1 litre (1¾ pint) jar or container

500g (1lb 2oz) garlic chives (buchu), trimmed
1 small carrot, julienned (optional)
1 spring onion, cut into matchsticks (optional)

FOR THE SEASONING PASTE

50g (1¾oz) gochugaru
2 tbsp anchovy fish sauce, or 2 tbsp kelp water with ½ tsp salt
30g (1oz) garlic, grated
30g (1oz) ginger, grated
50g (1¾oz) pear, grated (optional)
1 tbsp maesil-cheong (plum syrup), (for added fragrance, optional)
2–4 tbsp filtered water, to loosen paste, if needed

Kimmy's Notes

- **Chives:** Look for Korean or Asian garlic chives – flat, aromatic and stronger in flavour than common Western chives.
- **Heat level:** Buchu kimchi is meant to be bright and bold but reducing the gochugaru keeps it gentler.
- **Sweetness:** Grated pear balances the pungency, but can be omitted if you prefer.
- **Storage:** Keep chives pressed under their liquid and paste so the tops don't dry out.

Buchu kimchi, or garlic chive kimchi, is light, fragrant and quick to prepare. Traditionally made in spring when the first tender chives appear, it brings a fresh green punch and sharp aroma that mellows slightly after a short ferment.

This kimchi is typically eaten fresh within days, its crisp stems and bold flavour pair beautifully with grilled meats, rice or tucked into a ssam wrap with perilla leaves. Unlike cabbage kimchi, buchu kimchi is less about long ageing and more about capturing seasonal freshness at its peak

1. Prepare chives: Wash chives gently in cold water, rinsing thoroughly to remove any grit. Drain well. Cut into 5–7 cm (2–3in) lengths for easier mixing.

2. Make seasoning paste: In a large mixing bowl, combine gochugaru, fish sauce (or kelp water), garlic, ginger, grated pear and plum syrup, if using. Add a little water to loosen if needed. Stir into a paste and rest for 5 minutes to hydrate the chilli.

3. Combine: Add chives (and optional vegetables) to the bowl. Wearing gloves or using tongs, toss gently until evenly coated. Avoid squeezing – the stems should remain crisp.

4. Rest and wilt: Leave the seasoned chives at room temperature for 2–3 hours. They will soften, darken slightly and release liquid.

5. Pack and store: Transfer to a clean airtight container. Press down gently to remove air pockets and compact the chives. Leave 2cm (¾in) of headspace, wipe the rim and seal.

6. Ferment: You can eat this kimchi fresh on the same day, but flavour develops after 2–3 days in the fridge. Burp the container daily for the first 7 days. It keeps well for up to 2–3 weeks.

Serving Suggestions

- Serve with plain rice, grilled pork or beef, or tucked into ssam wraps with perilla leaves.
- Excellent as a topping for noodles or chopped into omelettes for a fragrant kick.

Baek Kimchi
백김치

VEGAN

Prep: 45 minutes
Brining: 4–5½ hours
Fermenting: 1–3 days at room temperature before refrigeration
Makes: 3–5 litre (5¼–8¾ pint) jar or container

2 medium napa cabbages (about 2kg/ 4lb 6oz total)
100–125g (3½–4½oz) coarse sea salt
500g (1lb 2oz) daikon, julienned
200g (7oz) firm pear, julienned
10 spring onions, cut into 7–8cm (3in) pieces
½–1 mild red, yellow or green bell pepper, thinly sliced (optional)

FOR THE SEASONING PASTE

1½ tbsp sweet rice flour or plain flour
1.4 litres (2½ pints) filtered water
70g (2½oz) garlic
70g (2½oz) ginger
100g (3½oz) carrot
30g (1oz) coarse salt

Serving Suggestions

- Cut into bite-size pieces and serve in small bowls with some of the brine.
- Enjoy some of the brine poured over rice or noodles or sip the broth directly as a refreshing palate cleanser.
- Best enjoyed when lightly tangy.

Kimmy's Notes

- **Clarity:** Strain the aromatic purée thoroughly for a clear broth.

Baek kimchi, or white kimchi, is the gentlest expression of traditional Korean fermentation. Made without gochugaru, it offers a clean, subtle flavour profile that highlights the natural sweetness of napa cabbage. Unlike its fiery red cousin, baek kimchi is mild, slightly fizzy when well fermented and often infused with aromatic fruits and vegetables.

Historically, this was the original form of kimchi before red chilli powder was introduced to Korea in the sixteenth century. Even after spicy kimchi gained popularity, baek kimchi remained cherished for its elegance and clarity, often served at royal tables or to elders, children and those sensitive to heat.

Baek kimchi ferments more quickly than red varieties and develops a refreshing, lightly tangy brine that's often sipped like a palate-cleansing broth. It is especially well-suited to winter, pairing beautifully with hot rice or simple soups.

1. Salt cabbage: Halve cabbages lengthways. Sprinkle salt between leaves and leave to brine for 4–5 hours, turning occasionally. Rinse two to three times in cold water, then drain in a colander for 30 minutes.

2. Cook porridge: Mix the flour with 100ml (3½fl oz) water until there are no lumps. In a medium saucepan, bring 750ml (1 pint 5fl oz) water to the boil, then whisk in the flour paste and cook for about 7–10 minutes until glossy. Leave to cool completely.

3. Blend aromatics: In a blender, put the, garlic, ginger, pear and 50ml (1¾fl oz) water and blend until smooth. Strain through a fine sieve and stir into cooled porridge. Discard anything left in the sieve. Add the salt and 500ml (17½fl oz) cold water to make a light broth. Stir until the salt has dissolved.

4. Assemble: Place drained cabbage halves in a clean container. Tuck julienned daikon, pear, spring onion and pepper, if using, between leaves. Pour broth over so the cabbages are fully submerged.

5. Ferment: Leave at room temperature for 1 day in the summer, 2 days in spring or autumn, or 3 days in winter before refrigerating. Burp the container daily for the first 7 days.

Chonggak Kimchi
총각김치

Prep: 40–50 minutes
Brining: 2–3 hours
Fermenting: 1–2 days at room temperature before refrigeration
Makes: 2 litre (3½ pint) jar

1kg (2lb 3oz) young radishes with tops
100g (3½oz) spring onions, diagonally sliced into 1–2cm (½in) pieces
50g (1¾oz) coarse sea salt
250ml (8¾fl oz) water
1 tsp glutinous rice flour

FOR THE SEASONING PASTE

60g (2oz) gochugaru
50ml (1¾fl oz) filtered water
50g (1¾oz) garlic, grated
50g (1¾oz) ginger, grated
30g (1oz) spring onion, roughly chopped
15g salted shrimp
2 tbsp anchovy fish sauce, or 2 tbsp kelp water with ½ tsp salt

---

Chonggak kimchi is one of Korea's most recognisable rustic kimchi styles, made with small young radishes known as chonggakmu and often called 'ponytail' radishes in English because of their long leafy tops. The name chonggak means 'bachelor', referring to how the slim radish with its tuft of greens resembles the traditional topknot hairstyle worn by young men in old Korea.

This kimchi brings together crunchy roots and tender greens in a bold, refreshing ferment. Its texture is wonderfully crisp, while the seasoning paste delivers layers of garlic, ginger, seafood umami and chilli warmth.

---

1. Clean vegetables: Trim and wash the radishes thoroughly, leaving greens intact if possible. Rinse spring onions.

2. Brine radishes: Dissolve the salt in the water. Soak radishes and sliced spring onions for 2–3 hours until slightly pliable.

3. Drain: Rinse well to remove excess salt, then drain thoroughly in a colander.

4. Make rice paste: In a small pan, whisk the glutinous rice flour with 4 tablespoons of water. Heat while stirring until thickened and smooth. Cool completely.

5. Prepare seasoning paste: In a large bowl, mix the gochugaru and water and leave for 5 minutes for the gochugaru to bloom. Add the garlic, ginger, spring onion, salted shrimp, fish sauce (or kelp water) and cooled rice paste, then gradually add salted water (4 tablespoons of water with ½ teaspoon of salt) until you have a thick paste. Taste and adjust salt if needed. At this stage the paste should taste a little saltier than you want in the final kimchi, with a balance of heat, garlic, ginger and savoury depth. The radishes will mellow and dilute the seasoning as they ferment.

6. Combine: Add the radishes, spring onions and watercress to the paste. Wearing gloves, gently mix by hand to coat everything evenly.

7. Pack jar: Arrange the seasoned radishes and vegetables neatly in a 1 litre jar. Press down firmly to remove air pockets. Leave 2cm (¾in) of headspace, wipe the rim and seal.

8. Ferment: Cover loosely and leave at 18–22°C (65–70°F) for 1–2 days until lightly fizzy and aromatic. Transfer to fridge to mature slowly. Burp the container daily for the first 7 days.

Serving Suggestions

- Remove one radish at a time and cut into bite-size pieces just before serving.
- Enjoy chilled with rice, grilled meats or a steaming bowl of soup.

Kimmy's Notes

- **Substitutes:** If true chonggakmu is unavailable, slender young daikon with leafy tops work well.
- **Fermentation:** Chonggak kimchi is best within the first 2–3 weeks, when the roots are crisp and the greens still retain texture.
- **Dry brining:** Traditional chonggak kimchi is often brined dry (just salted directly) rather than soaked in water brine as dry salting gives a better crunch. To do this, sprinkle about 3 percent of the radish weight in coarse salt (around 30g/1oz per 1kg/2lb 3oz) evenly over the roots and greens. Leave them at cool room temperature for 1½–2 hours, turning once or twice, until the radishes feel slightly softened but still crisp. Rinse well under cold water and drain thoroughly before seasoning.

Dongchimi
동치미

VEGAN

Prep: 45 minutes
Brining: 30-40 minutes
Fermenting: 2-3 days at room temperature, then 7-10 days in fridge for best flavour
Makes: 2-3 litre (3½-5¼ pint) jar

1kg (2lb 3oz) Korean radish (mu) or daikon, cut into 2.5 x 2.5 x 6cm (1 x 1 x 2½in long) batons
60g (2oz) coarse sea salt

FOR THE SEASONING PASTE

100g (3½oz) firm pear or sweet apple, sliced
70g (2½oz) garlic, halved
70g (2½oz) ginger, sliced
2 spring onions, cut into 5cm (2in) lengths
1-2 green chillies, slit lengthways (for aroma not heat, optional)
2-3 jujubes (dried Korean dates, optional)
10g (⅓oz) coarse salt
1.5 litres (2½ pints) cold water
2 tbsp grated pear (aids fermentation without overt sweetness, optional)

~~~~~

Dongchimi is a kimchi of quiet elegance. Unlike fiery red kimchi, this winter water kimchi is pale, mild and gently effervescent. Made with firm Korean radish (mu), pear or apple for sweetness, garlic, ginger, spring onions and, often, whole green chillies for fragrance rather than spice, it ferments into a brine that is faintly fizzy, lightly tangy and deeply refreshing, so clean it can be sipped like a tonic.

In Korea, dongchimi is tied to the rhythms of winter. Traditionally, it was prepared in large clay onggi jars and buried underground just before the first frost. Families would draw from the jar throughout the cold months, using the crisp brine as both a drink and a soup base. It was served with steamed rice, poured over noodles (dongchimi guksu), or enjoyed in small bowls to cleanse the palate before a heavy meal.

For many, dongchimi also carries memories. In my mother's kitchen, it was kept in the coldest corner of the house, waiting to soothe both stomach and spirit. She called it 'medicine for the gut and the mood'. Still, clear and quietly powerful, dongchimi is winter captured in a jar.

~~~~~

1. Prepare the radish: a medium radish (1kg/2lb 3oz) should give 16-20 batons. Wash and scrub the skin well; leave the peel on for flavour, but trim the ends. Slice into rectangular batons.

2. Pre-salt radish: Place the radish batons in a large bowl. Sprinkle with the salt, toss well and leave for 30-40 minutes, tossing once or twice. Drain but do not rinse.

3. Pack jar: Place a few pear or apple slices at the bottom of the jar. Layer in salted radish, garlic, ginger, spring onions, chilli and jujubes, if you like, until the jar is 80-90 percent full. Pack gently without crushing.

4. Make brine: Dissolve the salt in the water. Stir in the grated pear (if using), then pour into the jar until the ingredients are submerged, leaving 2cm (¾in) of headspace. Place a clean fermentation weight or ramekin on top to keep the radish below the brine.

5. Ferment: Cover loosely and leave at 16-20°C (61-68°F) for 2-3 days until tiny bubbles appear, the aroma turns

faintly sour and brine develops a light cloudiness – transfer to the fridge at this point. If the brine becomes opaque or gains a slimy texture then something has gone wrong (see Troubleshooting below).

6. Store: Leave in the fridge for 7–10 days before consuming, burping the jar daily. The brine should be fizzy and tangy, and the radish crisp. Over 2–3 weeks, the flavours will deepen while maintaining clarity.

Serving Suggestions

- Pour chilled broth into small bowls as a palate cleanser after rich dishes.
- Serve radish cubes alongside plain rice, grilled meat or fried foods.
- Use the brine as a base for kimchi-mari guksu (cold noodle soup).
- Sprinkle pine nuts or add thin pear slices as garnish for a traditional flourish.

Kimmy's Notes

- **Temperature:** Keep it cool; transfer to fridge after day 2 if your kitchen is warm.
- **Fizz:** A little natural carbonation is healthy – it should taste lively and refreshing.

Troubleshooting

Cloudy/slimy brine: Too warm, possible contamination or overpacked jar. Discard and restart.
No fizz: Leave at room temp for 1 more day.
Too salty: drain radish more thoroughly next time, or dilute broth slightly.
Overly sour: Shorten initial room-temperature fermentation stage.

Yeolmu Kimchi
열무김치

Prep: 25–35 minutes
Brining: 40–55 minutes
Fermenting: 12–24 hours at room temperature before refrigeration
Makes: 1.5–2 litre (2½–3½ pint) jar

500g (1lb 2oz) whole yeolmu (young summer radishes), or breakfast radishes with greens attached, or a mix of radish/turnip tops and tender salad radishes
45g (1½oz) coarse sea salt
1 litre (1¾ pints) cold water
300g (10½oz) Korean radish (mu) or firm daikon, cut into 3–4mm (⅛in) half-moons (optional)

FOR THE SEASONING PASTE

60–80g (2–2¾oz) gochugaru (60g/2oz for gentle heat; 80g/2¾oz for classic heat)
3 tbsp anchovy fish sauce, or 3 tbsp kelp water with ½ tsp salt
50g (1¾oz) garlic, grated
50g (1¾oz) ginger, grated
60g (2oz) pear or apple, grated (or 2 tbsp juice, optional)

~~~~~

Yeolmu kimchi is summer in a jar: juicy, lightly fizzy and wonderfully refreshing. Made with young radishes (yeolmu) that have tender greens, pale stems and small roots, it delivers a gentle crunch and a clean, cooling finish. Unlike winter ferments that favour depth and patience, this kimchi is quick, bright and best eaten young.

In Korea, it's the classic partner to chilled noodle bowls and a saviour on hot days, poured straight from the fridge over rice or noodles. The seasoning is red but restrained: gochugaru for colour and lift, garlic and ginger for backbone and a little seafood brine for savoury depth (with an easy vegan swap).
Keep it light, keep it cold and let the season speak through every chilled, juicy bite. This is kimchi at its most refreshing; alive with the rhythm of summer.

~~~~~

1. Prepare radishes: Discard any yellowed leaves and rinse the radishes well. Separate the greens and roots, and cut greens into 5–6 cm (2in) lengths. Trim the radish root tips. If they are finger-thin, leave whole. If they are thicker, cut lengthways into halves or quarters so all radish pieces are roughly the same thickness.

2. Pre-salt radishes: Toss the yeolmu greens, stems and roots with 15g (½oz) of the salt. Leave for 10 minutes to start wilting while preparing the brine.

3. Make brine: Dissolve the remaining 30g (1oz) of salt in the water to make a 3 percent brine. Submerge the yeolmu completely for 30–45 minutes, tossing once. Drain well in a colander over a bowl, reserving 500ml (17½fl oz) of the brine. Do not rinse the yeolmu.

4. Make seasoning paste: In a large bowl, combine the gochugaru, fish sauce (or kelp water), garlic, ginger and grated pear or apple. Rest for 5 minutes to hydrate the chilli.

5. Coat evenly: Wearing gloves, toss the yeolmu and the mu or daikon, if using, with the paste until evenly coated.

6. Adjust to 'summer brothy': Pour in 300–500ml (10½–17½fl oz) of the reserved brine to loosen the paste to a lightly pourable broth that's enough to just surround the vegetables.

7. Pack jar: Layer into the jar, pressing down to remove air gaps. Pour over the aromatic brine and top up with any more reserved brine or filtered water to cover the vegetables, if needed. Add a clean fermentation weight or ramekin to keep the veg submerged. Leave 2cm (¾in) of headspace, wipe the rim and seal lightly.

8. Ferment: Store the jar out of direct sunlight and between 18–20°C (65–68°F) for 12–24 hours, until tiny bubbles appear and a fresh lactic aroma develops, then transfer to the fridge. Burp the jar daily for the first 7 days.

9. Store: It is best between day 2–7 and will keep for 2–3 weeks, though the greens soften gradually.

Serving Suggestions

- Spoon generously over wheat noodles (yeolmu guksu); add ice for summer style.
- A cooling topping for hot rice, barley rice or some mixed grains.
- Cuts through fatty grilled pork or oily fish.
- Toss with cold tofu and sesame oil just before serving for a quick lunch.

Kimmy's Notes

- **To make it vegan:** Replace fish sauce with kelp water and a pinch of salt. Add an extra ½ tbsp of garlic for depth.
- **Broth tuning:** Too thick → add brine. Too salty → add cold water and thin pear slices.
- **Fast fermenter:** The greens will sour quickly; check it after 12 hours and refrigerate if necessary.

Troubleshooting

Flat broth: Paste too thick or under-salted. Add a little reserved brine or a pinch of salt if needed.
Too sour too fast: Move to fridge earlier next time; serve over ice.
Slimy texture: Too warm or overpacked; discard and keep cooler next time.
Leaves floating/drying: Add clean weight; top up with reserved brine.

Oi-sobagi
오이소박이

Prep: 45–60 minutes
Brining: 30–40 minutes
Fermenting: Up to 1 day (to taste)
Makes: 2–3 litre (3½–5¼ pint) container

1kg (2lb 3oz) Korean cucumbers, (or firm mini/Persian cucumbers)
50g (1¾oz) coarse sea salt
1 litre (1¾ pints) water
100g (3½oz) garlic chives, cut into 5cm (2in) lengths
100g (3½oz) carrots, julienned

FOR THE SEASONING PASTE

100g (3½oz) gochugaru
2 tbsp anchovy fish sauce, or 2 tbsp kelp water with ½ tsp salt
50g (1¾oz) pear or apple, grated
50g (1¾oz) garlic, grated

~~~

Oi-sobagi is summer kimchi at its most refreshing. Crisp cucumbers stuffed with a vibrant mix of chives, carrots and aromatic seasonings. The name sobagi means 'stuffed' and the cucumbers are slit and filled with a colourful kimchi paste so that every bite bursts with flavour. Oi-sobagi was once made to revive appetites during Korea's hot, humid summers. Cucumbers are naturally cooling and hydrating, while garlic chives are known for their warming, digestive properties, which together forming a perfectly balanced summer side dish.

Unlike long-fermented cabbage kimchi, this one is made to be eaten fresh while the cucumbers are still juicy and crunchy. The trick is in the salting: hot brine softens the cucumbers just enough without making them mushy, so they keep their snap even after the seasoning has seeped in

~~~

1. Prepare the cucumbers: Wash thoroughly and trim both ends. Cut into 7–10cm (3–4in) lengths. Slice each piece with a deep cross-shaped slit, stopping 1cm (½in) from the end so they stay intact.

2. Make hot brine: Dissolve the salt in the water and bring to a boil. Place cucumbers in a deep-sided tray, pour the hot brine over, and weigh them down with a plate. Leave for 30–40 minutes, turning once. The cucumbers should soften slightly but remain firm.

3. Prepare stuffing: Slice garlic chives and carrots into thin matchsticks. In a large bowl, combine the gochugaru, fish sauce (or kelp water), grated pear or apple and the garlic. Add the vegetables and toss until evenly coated.

4. Drain cucumbers: Discard the brine, but do not rinse the cucumbers. Pat them gently with kitchen paper to remove excess moisture.

5. Stuff the cucumbers: Gently open each slit and pack generously with stuffing. Place cucumbers into a clean container, layering any leftover stuffing.

6. Fermentation: Unlike cabbage kimchi, oi-sobagi is not meant for long storage – enjoy it while the cucumbers are still crisp. For a fresh taste, refrigerate and serve after a few hours. For a light tang, leave at cool room temperature (18–20°C/65–68°F) for 12–24 hours before

refrigerating. Burp the container daily and eat within 5–7 days.

~~~

Serving Suggestions

- Simply paired with a bowl of steamed rice.
- Alongside cold noodle dishes (such as naengmyeon or bibim guksu).
- With grilled meats or barbecue for contrast.
- As a crisp, cooling side to spicy stews.
- Packed into lunchboxes or picnic meals for a refreshing bite.

~~~

Kimmy's Notes

- **Salt balance:** The stuffing should taste slightly salty on its own; once combined with cucumbers, the flavour balances.

~~~

Troubleshooting

Too soft: Brined too long; reduce the time to 20–30 minutes.
Too salty: Rinse cucumbers lightly after brining.
Bland: Add an extra ½ tablespoon of fish sauce or a pinch of salt to stuffing.

Geotjeori
겉절이

Prep: 30–40 minutes
Brining: 30–60 minutes
Fermenting: None (best eaten fresh, but can rest 1–2 days chilled)
Makes: 2 litre (3½ pint) container

1kg (2lb 3oz) napa cabbage
70–80g (2½oz) coarse sea salt
250ml (8¾fl oz) water
300g (10½oz) Korean radish (mu) or daikon, julienned (optional)
300g (10½oz) garlic chives, cut into 5cm (2in) lengths (optional)

FOR THE SEASONING PASTE

100g (3½oz) gochugaru
2 tbsp anchovy fish sauce, or 2 tbsp kelp water with ½ tsp salt
50g (1¾oz) grated pear (or 1 tbsp sugar)
50g (1¾oz) garlic, grated
50g (1¾oz) ginger, grated

Geotjeori is essentially a fresh kimchi with napa cabbage, seasoned lightly and eaten raw or after just a short rest. This style is not suitable for long storage and is meant to be eaten soon after preparation. This allows the natural sweetness and crispness of the cabbage to immediately shine through, bright and refreshing.

Across Korea, it goes by many names: in Jeonju it's called saengji (생지); in Gyeongsang-do, nal kimchi (날김치). No matter the name, its role is the same – a quick, intuitive side dish that adds freshness to the table. Families prepare it in countless variations: some enrich it with salted shrimp or anchovy fish sauce, while others prefer a vegan style.

1. Prepare cabbage: Trim the root, and slice the cabbage in half lengthways. Cut into pieces along the leaf veins so each piece contains both stem and leaf. Rinse lightly in cold water to help the salt stick.

2. Salt cabbage: In a large bowl, layer the cabbage and sprinkle with the salt as you go. Pour the water over the top to help dissolve the salt. Leave for 30–60 minutes, turning once or twice. It will need less time in the summer, and a bit longer if it is cold. Bend a thick stem piece – if it folds without breaking and feels supple, it's ready.

3. Rinse and drain: Rinse the cabbage three times in cold water to remove excess salt and drain thoroughly in a colander.

4. Prepare radish (optional): Peel and julienne the mu or daikon, if using. Add directly to the drained cabbage.

5. Make seasoning paste: In the large bowl, combine the gochugaru, fish sauce (or kelp water), grated pear (or sugar), garlic and ginger.

6. Mix cabbage with paste: Add the vegetables to the paste and, wearing gloves, gently mix until they are evenly coated.

7. Add chives (optional): Toss in the garlic chives, if using, at the end to keep them fresh and crisp.

8. Pack and serve: Transfer to a container, pressing down lightly to remove air pockets. Geotjeori is best eaten immediately or kept in the fridge and eaten within 1–2 days.

Serving Suggestions

- Serve fresh alongside hot rice for a crisp, spicy bite.
- Pair with stews (jjigae) or soups for balance.
- Add as a side to grilled meats, fish or tofu dishes.

Kimmy's Tips

- **For a lighter flavour,** reduce the gochugaru and increase the radish for crunch.
- **If the kimchi tastes too salty,** rinse the cabbage once more and let it rest with a little extra pear juice.
- **If using a blender to make the paste,** just the grated pear (and juice) may be insufficient to work it, so add the same amount of water as pear for better results.
- **Goetjeori is not intended to be fermented** and is normally eaten within the first few days of making, if not immediately. It will not keep and will usually spoil within a week.

Gaji Kimchi
가지 김치

Prep: 20–30 minutes
Brining: 1¼ hours
Fermenting: 12–18 hours at room temperature before refrigeration
Makes: 3 litre (5¼ pint) jar

1kg (2lb 3oz) Korean, Japanese or UK aubergines (8–10 slender, about 15cm/6in long)
100g (3½oz) coarse sea salt
2 litres (3½ pints) water
80–100g (3–3½oz) spring onions, sliced
70g (2½oz) Korean radish (mu), julienned
70g (2½oz) carrot, julienne

FOR THE SEASONING PASTE

100g (3½oz) gochugaru
3 tbsp anchovy fish sauce, or 3 tbsp kelp water with ½ tsp salt
50g (1¾oz) garlic, grated
50g (1¾oz) ginger, grated
50g (1¾oz) pear, grated

Gaji kimchi is a kimchi made with aubergine. It's soft, savoury and fleeting – a summer delicacy made when tender aubergines are abundant. The aubergines are brined, lightly steamed until pliable, then dressed in a spicy seasoning paste that they quickly soak up. Gaji kimchi shows that kimchi doesn't always mean crunch. Sometimes, it means velvety texture and deep flavour. Part of Korea's quick-ferment kimchi family (alongside oi-sobagi on page 76 and yeolmu kimchi on page 74), gaji kimchi is designed for immediacy. Its soft flesh absorbs seasoning like a sponge, creating bold flavour in very little time. Traditionally enjoyed in the warmer months, it's a side dish that pairs beautifully with rice, noodles, grilled fish or tofu.

---

1. Prepare and brine aubergines: First wash the aubergines and trim off their stems. Halve or quarter lengthways. If using a thicker variety of aubergine, cut each half into three strips. In a large bowl, dissolve the salt in the water. Soak aubergines in the brine for 30 minutes, then drain thoroughly.

2. Steam and cool: In a steamer over a pan of simmering water, steam the drained aubergines for 5–6 minutes, until pliable. Be careful not over-steam as this can lead to mushiness. They should bend easily but not collapse. Spread out on a cooling rack and allow to cool for about 30 minutes.

3. Make seasoning paste: In a large bowl, mix the gochugaru, fish sauce (or kelp water), garlic, ginger and grated pear. Add the spring onions, radish and carrot. Toss until well coated. If it seems too dry, add 1–2 tablespoons of water.

4. Season aubergines: Handling them lightly as they are delicate, toss the cooled aubergines with the seasoning paste until well coated. If an aubergine splits, tuck seasoning inside.

5. Ferment and store: Pack the aubergines gently into a clean jar, leaving about 2cm (¾in) of headspace at the top. Wipe the rim and seal and leave at room temperature for 12–18 hours until lightly tangy. Refrigerate and enjoy within 3–5 days. Burp the jar daily.

Serving Suggestions

- Serve whole or slice into bite-size pieces.
- Sprinkle with sesame seeds and drizzle with sesame oil before serving.
- Pair with hot rice, soups, grilled fish or tofu dishes.

~~~~~~~

Kimmy's Notes

- **Aubergines:** Korean and Japanese aubergines are quite slender varieties. If they cannot be sourced, whatever is available locally can be used
- **Fermentation stages:**
    - Fresh (immediate): Soft, savoury, gently spicy.
    - Lightly sour (12–18 hrs): Tangier, tender bite.
    - Later (3–5 days refrigerated): Softer, with deeper umami.

~~~~~~~

Troubleshooting

Flat broth: Too mushy: Steamed too long/fermented too warm → steam less, refrigerate earlier.
Too salty: Rinse aubergines lightly after brining.
Not enough flavour: Increase quantity of seasoning paste – aubergines absorb it readily.

Kkaennip Kimchi
깻잎김치

Prep: 20–40 minutes
Fermentation: 4–6 hours at cool room temperature before refrigeration
Makes: 1 litre (1¾ pint) container

80–100 perilla leaves (about 150–180g/ 5¼–6¼oz), washed and thoroughly dried

FOR THE SEASONING PASTE

30g (1oz) gochugaru
2 tbsp anchovy fish sauce, or 2 tbsp kelp water with ½ tsp salt
20g (¾oz) garlic, grated
20g (¾oz) ginger, grated
30g (1oz) spring onions, cut into 3cm (1in) pieces
4 tbsp pear juice
20g (¾oz) rice syrup

Serving Suggestions

- Wrap around warm rice for a simple bite.
- Tuck into bibimbap for herbal depth.
- Pair with grilled meats, fish, or tofu.
- Add to a lunchbox for a fragrant side dish.

Kimmy's Notes

- **Vegan flavour depth:** Replace plain kelp water with kelp and dried shiitake stock and add ½ tablespoon extra sesame oil.
- **Dry leaves well:** If damp, the paste will turn watery and shorten shelf life.
- **Too salty:** Mix in 1 tablespoon each of pear and onion juice.

Kkaennip kimchi is one of the simplest yet most aromatic banchan. Tender perilla leaves are stacked and brushed with a fragrant paste, then left to rest so the flavours meld. Earthy, herbal and lightly spicy, each leaf becomes a ready-made wrap for warm rice, grilled meats or mixed grains.

Traditionally, a seafood-based seasoning is used, with anchovy sauce and salted shrimp lending deep savoury notes and a longer shelf life. A more recent development has been the inclusion of sesame seeds and oil. While they have long been part of Korean cooking, their consistent use in kkaennip kimchi only became standard in the last century. Their inclusion deepens the flavour and fragrance, making the kimchi nuttier and richer.

A vegan version swaps in kelp water and a little extra salt for a clean, plant-based flavour that highlights the natural aroma of the leaves. Which ever version you choose, kkaennip kimchi is quick to make, easy to store and delivers maximum flavour in every fold.

1. Make the paste: In a bowl, combine gochugaru, fish sauce (or kelp water) garlic, ginger, spring onions, pear juice and rice syrup. Mix until a thick, spreadable paste forms.

2. Layer and season: Take 5–6 perilla leaves at a time. Spread ½–1 teaspoon of paste on each leaf, alternating the stem direction as you stack. Continue until all leaves are coated.

3. Pack: Place the stacked leaves neatly in a clean container, pressing gently to remove air pockets. Spread any leftover paste over the top.

4. Ferment: Leave at cool room temperature (18–20°C/65–68°F) for 4–6 hours, then refrigerate.

5. Store: Press down leaves if liquid rises to minimise air pockets. They are best eaten within 1–10 days for the seafood version, or 1–7 days for the vegan version, for peak freshness.

Mu Mallaengi Kimchi
무말랭이김치

Prep: 35–45 minutes
Fermentation: Up to 2 days at room temperature (optional)
Makes: 1 litre (1¾ pint) container

200g (7oz) dried shredded radish (mu malraengi)

FOR THE SEASONING PASTE

100g (3½oz) gochugaru
2 tbsp anchovy fish sauce, or 2 tbsp kelp water with ½ tsp salt
30g (1oz) garlic, grated
30g (1oz) ginger, grated
30g (1oz) rice syrup
200ml (7fl oz) filtered water

Kimmy's Notes

- **Texture:** Dried radish remains pleasantly chewy even after weeks in the fridge.
- **Salt balance:** Less salt is needed than in fresh radish kimchi, since the flavour is concentrated.

The name mu-mallaengi kimchi comes directly from its ingredients: mu (radish) and mallaengi (sun-dried), proving that nothing in a Korean kitchen goes to waste. Made from sun-dried radish strips, it delivers concentrated flavour and a satisfying chew that contrasts beautifully with rice or soup. The drying process intensifies the radish's natural sweetness and aroma, so when it's rehydrated and seasoned, each strand carries bold, tangy and slightly elastic character.

Traditionally, this kimchi was made in late autumn after kimjang, using leftover radishes that weren't salted for whole-cabbage kimchi. Its excellent keeping quality made it a practical winter side dish, slowly softening and developing savoury depth in storage.

1. Rehydrate radish: Place the dried shredded radish in a large bowl and cover with cold water, soaking for 20–30 minutes until plump and pliable. Drain well and cut into 4cm (1½in) lengths.

2. Make seasoning paste: In the same large bowl, combine the gochugaru, fish sauce (or kelp water), garlic, ginger, rice syrup and filtered water. Mix to form a thick, even paste.

3. Mix and coat: Add the drained radish to the seasoning paste then, wearing gloves, massage the paste thoroughly into the radish until every strand is evenly coated.

4. Pack and ferment: Transfer the seasoned radish into an airtight container, pressing down to remove air pockets. For fresh, crisp flavour serve immediately. Otherwise, for a tangier depth, leave at room temperature for 1–2 days before refrigerating.

5. Store: Burp the container daily for the first 7 days. It will keep for 3–4 weeks in the fridge; the flavours will deepen over time.

Serving Suggestions

- Serve as a side dish with warm rice.
- Pack into lunchboxes for a chewy, flavourful banchan.
- Pair with grilled fish, soups or stews for a savoury counterpoint.

A Year of Ferments

Kimchi does not stand still. Like the seasons, it shifts – sometimes raw and green, sometimes deep and slow, sometimes cooling, sometimes warming. In Korea, kimchi has always followed nature's rhythm. What is planted in spring, gathered in summer, stored in autumn and survived on in winter shapes what goes into the jar.

The beauty of kimchi is that it is never just one recipe. It is a cycle, a rhythm, a way of eating that responds to both body and land. This chapter traces that rhythm through the four seasons and shows how kimchi can be traditional and adaptable, whether you are in Seoul, London or anywhere else in the world.

THE CYCLE – ALIVE & ONGOING

Kimchi is never finished. It shifts with the seasons, just as it shifts with days in the jar. What is raw today may be perfectly balanced tomorrow, deeply sour next week, and mellow in a stew a month later. The same principle that guides a single jar guides the whole year: change is not a flaw but the essence of kimchi.

Spring renews, summer refreshes, autumn sustains and winter comforts. Through this cycle, kimchi becomes more than food – it becomes a way of living in rhythm with the world, season by season.

SPRING – FRESH & GREEN

In Korea, spring is the season of emergence. Snow softens, shoots break through the soil, and markets brim with tender greens, sharp with life and full of vitality. After months of winter preservation, kimchi takes a lighter turn. These jars are not for storage but for renewal: ferments that wake the body, as fleeting as the season itself.

Spring is the time for geotjeori (fresh, unfermented kimchi) and quick ferments made from young napa cabbage, wild herbs and foraged greens. They are eaten within days, their bitterness and crunch a signal that winter is over and strength is returning. Seasonings stay simple, with garlic, ginger and chilli used sparingly to lift rather than mask the vegetables.

Spring kimchi is defined by its clean, raw brightness. Fermentation happens gently, often tasting best after just a day or two. These greens are nutrient-rich, slightly bitter and mineral-heavy, replenishing the body after the cold.

Here you'll find recipes that capture this spirit of renewal: crisp, refreshing and young.

Broccoli Kimchi

Prep: 25 minutes
Brining: 20–30 minutes
Fermentation: 1–2 days at room temperature before refrigeration
Makes: 1 litre (1¾ pint) jar

200g (7oz) broccoli (about 1 medium head), cut into bite-size florets and 1cm (½in) thick stem slices
100g (3½oz) daikon, cut into matchsticks
15g (½oz) coarse sea salt

FOR THE SEASONING PASTE

10g (⅓oz) gochugaru
2 tbsp anchovy fish sauce, or 2 tbsp kelp water with ½ tsp salt
2 garlic cloves, grated
2.5cm (1in) ginger, grated
1 small spring onion, sliced into 2cm (½in) lengths

Kimmy's Notes

- **Texture:** Broccoli will stay crisp but will gradually soften in the fridge over time.
- **Fermentation:** Warmer kitchens may shorten the fermentation to just 1 day.

Bright green, slightly bitter and beautifully briny, this is a crunchy twist on classic kimchi.

This vibrant kimchi highlights broccoli's firm florets and crisp stems. The broccoli stays tender-crisp, while the gochugaru and garlic infuse it with depth. It's an excellent way to enjoy extra greens as a probiotic-packed banchan or salad topper.

1. Salt vegetables: In a large bowl, toss the broccoli florets and daikon matchsticks with the salt. Leave for 20–30 minutes until softened and lightly wilted. Drain thoroughly in a colander, reserving a little of the brine.

2. Prepare seasoning paste: In the same large bowl, mix the gochugaru, fish sauce (or kelp water), garlic and ginger into a paste. Thin with 1–2 teaspoons of the reserved brine if too stiff.

3. Mix and coat: Add drained broccoli and daikon to the paste with spring onion. Wearing gloves, gently massage the paste in until the broccoli and daikon are evenly coated.

4. Pack jar: Transfer to a clean jar, pressing down to remove air pockets. Leave about 2cm (¾in) of headspace. Pour over any remaining paste or liquid, wipe the rim and seal.

5. Ferment and store: Ferment at room temperature (18–22°C/65–70°F) for 1–2 days, tasting daily. Once it reaches your preferred level of tang, seal tightly and refrigerate for up to 2 weeks. Burp the jar daily for the first 7 days.

Serving Suggestions

- Serve chilled as a crunchy side with rice or grilled protein.
- Add to salads or grain bowls for tangy contrast.
- Stir into fried rice or noodles just before serving.

Wild Garlic Kimchi

Prep time: 20 minutes
Brining: 15–30 minutes
Fermentation: 1–2 days at room temperature before refrigeration
Makes: 1 litre (1¾ pint) jar

500–800g (1lb 2oz–1lb 12oz) wild garlic (ramsons/ramps)
200g (7oz) daikon, julienned (optional)
30g (1oz) coarse sea salt

FOR THE SEASONING PASTE

50–100g (2–3½oz) gochugaru, depending on taste
40g (1½oz) garlic, grated (optional)
40g (1½oz) ginger, grated
2 tbsp anchovy fish sauce, or 2 tbsp kelp water with ½ tsp salt
50g (1¾oz) Asian pear, grated

Wild garlic kimchi captures the vibrant aroma of spring. Also known as ramsons in the UK and ramps in North America, wild garlic brings a bold fragrance and fresh bite to the table. When lightly fermented, its pungency mellows into a bright, herbal tang that pairs beautifully with the chilli-spiced seasoning.

Traditionally, quick greens like wild garlic (maneulip in Korean, when cultivated) are enjoyed in early spring, often mixed with radish or chives for a lively banchan. This kimchi is best eaten young: still bright and aromatic within the first week, while the leaves retain their tender texture. It also adapts wonderfully into fusion cooking – stirred through warm rice, tossed with noodles or even added to pasta for a garlicky kick.

1. Wash and prep: Trim and wash the wild garlic. Shake off excess water and leave to drain for 5–10 minutes, giving a final shake after.

2. Salting: Place the wild garlic and daikon (if using) into a bowl and toss with the salt. Leave for 15–30 minutes until the wild garlic leaves look wilted and have released some liquid. Drain, reserving 1–2 tablespoons of the brine.

3. Make seasoning paste: In the same bowl, combine the gochugaru, garlic, if using, ginger, fish sauce (or kelp water) and grated pear. Adjust the consistency with a splash of the reserved brine if too thick.

4. Mix: Add the drained wild garlic to the bowl. Wearing gloves, gently massage the leaves with the seasoning until evenly coated.

5. Jar and ferment: Pack into a clean jar, pressing down to remove air pockets. Leave about 2cm (¾in) of headspace, wipe the rim and then seal and ferment at room temperature for 1–2 days, tasting daily. Once pleasantly tangy, tighten the lid and refrigerate. For a fresh taste, it's best enjoyed within the first 3–5 days, but the flavour deepens and becomes more punchy over a longer period.

6. Storage: Burp the jar daily for the first 7 days. Keep in the fridge for up to 3 weeks to develop a deeper and more mature flavour, though the leaves lose their springy bite after about a week.

Serving Suggestions

• Serve as a zesty side at barbecues with beef, pork or well-seasoned chicken.
• Stir through warm rice or noodles for an instant flavour boost.
• Chop and scatter over salads or avocado toast for a garlicky punch.

Kimmy's Notes

• **Substitutions:** If Asian pear isn't available, then use sweet apple or a firm Western pear.
• **Vegan flavour depth:** Use kelp and shiitake mushroom stock instead of kelp water alone.

Troubleshooting

Too salty: Rinse the greens more thoroughly before mixing with paste.
Too mild: Increase gochugaru or add an extra clove of garlic.
Paste too runny: Add an extra spoonful of gochugaru, and omit brine.

Min-deul-le (Dandelion) Kimchi
민들레 김치

Prep: 20–25 minutes
Brining: 20–30 minutes
Fermentation: 1–2 days at room temperature before refrigeration

300g (10½oz) young dandelion greens, washed and trimmed
300g (10½oz) daikon, cut into thin matchsticks
30g (1oz) coarse sea salt

FOR THE SEASONING PASTE

30g (1oz) gochugaru (about 2 tbsp)
2 tbsp anchovy fish sauce, or 2 tbsp kelp water with ½ tsp salt
30g (1oz) garlic, grated
30g (1oz) ginger, grated
15g (½oz) spring onions, cut into 2cm (¾in) pieces

Dandelion greens are often overlooked as weeds, yet in Korea they have long been valued for their healing properties, especially in spring when the body craves cleansing and renewal after a long winter. Young dandelion leaves carry a grassy, slightly bitter taste that softens beautifully through fermentation, gaining a rounded, tangy depth. This kimchi is deeply seasonal and best when the leaves are tender, making it an ideal way to honour early spring.

Dandelion kimchi is light, sharp and short-lived. Its bitterness, balanced by garlic and gochugaru, pairs well with the richness of grilled meat or oily fish, cutting through any heaviness with a fresh bite. In rice bowls or bibimbap, it acts as a lively accent. The bitterness that might deter some is exactly what makes this kimchi so intriguing: it awakens the palate, reminding us that not all ferments must be sweet or mellow.

1. Salt vegetables: Place the dandelion greens and daikon into a large bowl. Sprinkle over the coarse salt and toss gently to coat. Leave for 20–30 minutes, tossing halfway. The greens will wilt and release liquid. Drain thoroughly in a colander, reserving a little of the brine.

2. Prepare seasoning paste: In the same bowl, mix together the gochugaru, fish sauce (or kelp water), garlic and ginger. If the paste is too thick to spread, add 1–2 teaspoons of the reserved brine until smooth and spreadable.

3. Mix and coat: Add the drained dandelion and daikon to the bowl with the paste, then add the spring onion. Wearing gloves, gently massage the paste into the greens until evenly coated. Take care not to bruise the leaves excessively, as they are delicate.

4. Pack jar: Transfer the seasoned greens into a clean jar. Press down gently to remove air pockets. Pour in any remaining paste and liquid to cover the vegetables, leaving about 2cm (¾in) of headspace at the top. Wipe the rim and seal.

5. Ferment: Leave at room temperature (18–22°C/65–70°F) for 1–2 days. Check daily, pressing down to keep the greens submerged. Taste to monitor sourness. Once it reaches your preferred level of tang, seal tightly and refrigerate. Burp the jar daily, and eat within 1 week

as the flavour sharpens and the bitterness intensifies if kept longer.

Serving Suggestions

- Serve chilled as a bright, zingy side dish with rice.
- Stir through bibimbap or warm grain bowls for added contrast.
- Pair with grilled fish or rich meat to balance with a clean, bitter-tangy bite.
- Add a few spoonfuls of the brine to dress salads or noodle dishes for a fermented kick.

Kimmy's Notes

- **Bitterness:** Young dandelion greens in early spring are less bitter and more tender. If using older leaves, blanch briefly in boiling water, cool and squeeze dry before salting.
- **Fermentation speed:** In warmer kitchens, the greens will ferment rapidly – often in just 24 hours. In cooler kitchens you may need to allow 2–3 days.
- **Local sourcing:** In the UK, dandelion leaves sometimes appear in spring markets, or they can be foraged from clean, untreated areas. Choose leaves from young plants, ideally smaller than 15cm (6in).

Asparagus-chive Kimchi

Prep time: 20 minutes
Brining: 20–25 minutes
Fermentation: 1–3 days at room temperature before refrigeration
Makes: 1 litre (1¾ pint) jar

400g (14oz) asparagus, trimmed and cut lengthways into halves then quarters (if especially thick)
100g (3½oz) garlic chives (or regular chives if unavailable), cut into 4cm (1½in) lengths
20g (¾oz) coarse sea salt

FOR THE SEASONING PASTE

40g (1½oz) gochugaru
2 tbsp anchovy fish sauce, or 2 tbsp kelp water with ½ tsp salt
30g (1oz) garlic, grated
30g (1oz) ginger, grated
50g (1¾oz) pear or apple, grated (optional)
1 spring onion, finely sliced

Kimmy's Notes

- **Seasonality:** While asparagus is generally available all year round from supermarkets, it is best in spring when at its tender peak.
- **Crunch:** Eat sooner for maximum crispness as it will soften with age.

Troubleshooting

Too salty: Rinse asparagus briefly after the salt and drain step.
Too mild: Add extra gochugaru or more garlic.

Asparagus-chive kimchi is a modern, seasonal twist on Korea's classic vegetable ferments. Tender asparagus spears bring a grassy freshness, while garlic chives add a subtle perfume and a touch of bite. Unlike long-fermented cabbage kimchi, this version is meant to be enjoyed young, when the asparagus still retains its crunch and vivid green colour. A short fermentation of just a few days softens the raw edge, leaving a lightly tangy, aromatic side that captures the essence of spring. Served alongside rice, grilled fish or tucked into a lunchbox, it's a refreshing kimchi that celebrates the fleeting season.

1. Salt asparagus: Place the asparagus pieces in a large bowl, sprinkle with the sea salt, and toss well. Leave for 20–25 minutes, turning occasionally, until they release water and bend slightly without snapping. Drain, reserving a few spoonfuls of the brine.

2. Prepare the paste: In the same large bowl, mix the gochugaru, fish sauce (or kelp water), garlic, ginger, grated pear or apple, if using, and spring onion. Stir in 1–2 tablespoons of the reserved brine to form a loose paste.

3. Combine: Add the salted asparagus and chives to the paste. Wearing gloves, gently toss the veg in the paste until evenly coated.

4. Jar: Pack the mixture into a clean jar, pressing down gently to remove air pockets. Pour in any remaining paste and brine so the vegetables are lightly coated and seal.

5. Ferment: Leave at room temperature (18–22°C/65–70°F) for 1–3 days, depending on the warmth of your kitchen. Taste daily and when the asparagus develops a light tang but still retains its crunch, transfer to the fridge.

6. Store: Best eaten within 1–2 weeks, while the flavours are fresh and bright. Burp the jar daily for the first 7 days.

Serving Suggestions

- Serve as a light side to rice and grilled fish.
- Chop and toss into noodle salads for a springtime kick.
- Add to sandwiches or wraps for freshness and gentle spice.

Morkovcha-inspired Carrot Kimchi
모르콥차 김치

Prep: 30 minutes
Brining: 30 minutes
Fermentation: 2–3 days at room temperature before refrigeration
Makes: 1 litre (1¾ pint) jar

500g (1lb 2oz) carrots, julienned
1 small red onion (about 80g/2¾oz), thinly sliced into half-moons
20g (¾oz) coarse sea salt

FOR THE SEASONING PASTE

15g (½oz) gochugaru
2 tbsp anchovy fish sauce, or 2 tbsp kelp water with ½ tsp salt
30g (1oz) garlic, grated
15g (½oz) ginger, grated
1 tsp ground coriander (freshly ground if possible)

Kimmy's Notes

- **Prep:** Morkovcha kimchi works best with carrots cut thin and even – a julienne peeler or mandolin will save time and create the right crunch. For an even more traditional Korean-Uzbek aroma, finish with a pinch of ground black pepper, fresh dill and finely chopped coriander leaves.
- **Texture:** Carrots hold their crunch longer than cabbage, but their snappy texture works well for quick-ferment kimchi, too.
- **Spice profile:** Ground coriander is the key for authenticity, so don't skip it. Freshly ground seeds have far more fragrance.

This kimchi takes inspiration from morkovcha, a beloved Korean-Uzbek carrot salad created by the Koryo-saram (ethnic Koreans in Central Asia. Traditionally seasoned with garlic, coriander, vinegar and oil, morkovcha was a way to preserve Korean flavours in a new land where napa cabbage wasn't always available. This version brings the best of both worlds together: the sweet crunch of carrots paired with the lactic tang of kimchi fermentation. Unlike classic morkovcha, this version omits vinegar and oil so natural fermentation can take place. The result is bold, aromatic and versatile.

1. Salt vegetables: Place the julienned carrots and onion into a large bowl. Sprinkle with the sea salt and toss gently. Leave for 30 minutes, tossing once or twice, until softened and releasing liquid. Drain, reserving the brine, but do not rinse.

2. Prepare seasoning paste: In the same large bowl, combine gochugaru, fish sauce (or kelp water) garlic, ginger and ground coriander. Stir to a smooth paste. Loosen the paste with 1–2 teaspoons of the drained brine, if needed.

3. Mix and coat: Add the drained vegetables to the paste. Wearing gloves, massage gently until the carrot matchsticks and onion slices are evenly coated with spice.

4. Pack jar: Transfer to a clean jar, pressing down to remove air pockets. Pour over any remaining paste or liquid. Leave about 2cm (¾in) of headspace, wipe the rim and seal.

5. Ferment and store: Leave at room temperature (18–22°C/65–70°F) for 2–3 days. Check daily, the carrots will develop a slight fizz and tang. Once fermented to your taste, tighten the lid and refrigerate. Burp the jar daily for the first 7 days, and eat within 2 weeks.

Serving Suggestions

- Enjoy as a crisp banchan alongside rice and grilled meat.
- Add to wraps, tacos or sandwiches for tang and crunch.
- Toss into salads for colour and spice.
- Pair with lamb kebabs or roasted aubergines for a Korean-Uzbek fusion plate.

SUMMER – CRUNCHY & BRIGHT

In Korea, summer kimchi has never been about storage. When the air turns heavy and the windows stay open, what people wanted were jars that refreshed the body: crisp cucumbers, sun-warmed tomatoes, tender courgettes and fragrant herbs. These were made in small batches, ready within a day or two, eaten straight from the fridge to restore energy in the heat.

Summer ferments are fast. Warm air accelerates lactic acid bacteria activity, so flavours develop overnight and can quickly turn sharp. Jars must be checked daily, the line between perfectly refreshing and overly sour passing in a flash. Seasonings are lighter too, with less salt to keep flavours bright and hydrating, the vegetables themselves providing crispness and cool relief.

In this section, you'll find recipes that embody summer's brightness: juicy, refreshing and best eaten young, a burst of cool relief in the hottest months.

Chopped Oi Kimchi
오이김치

Prep: 25 minutes
Brining: 30 minutes
Fermentation: 1–2 days at room temperature before refrigeration
Makes: 1 litre (1¾ pint) jar

800g (1lb 12oz) Korean cucumbers (or firm mini/Persian cucumbers)
30g (1oz) coarse salt
1 large red onion or 2 medium onions, cut into medium chunks
50g (1¾oz) garlic chives, cut into 5cm (2in) pieces
50g (1¾oz) spring onions, cut into 5cm (2in) pieces
10–15g (½oz) red chilli, thinly sliced (optional, for colour and heat)

FOR THE SEASONING PASTE

50g (1¾oz) gochugaru, or to taste
4 tbsp anchovy fish sauce, or 4 tbsp kelp water with ½ tsp salt
30g (1oz) garlic, grated
30g (1oz) ginger, grated
50g (1¾oz) Asian pear or apple, grated
2 tbsp maesil-cheong (plum syrup), or 1 tbsp sugar and 1½ tbsp water
2 tbsp kelp water or water

Kimmy's Notes

• **Cucumber choice:** Korean, Persian or mini cucumbers are best; English cucumbers can be used if halved lengthways, deseeded and sliced into 1cm (½in) half-moons.
• **Sweetness balance:** Asian pear gives the most authentic flavour, but sweet apple or Western pear works well.
• **Fermentation speed:** In warm kitchens, cucumbers may sour within 24 hours, so taste regularly.

Oi kimchi is the taste of summer in a jar: crisp, refreshing and satisfyingly spicy. Unlike the oi-sobagi (stuffed cucumber kimchi) on page 76, which requires careful splitting and filling, this chopped style is simpler and quicker – ready to enjoy in under an hour or within a few days, before the cucumbers soften too much. The cucumbers remain snappy and full of water, while the seasoning paste clings to every bite, infusing each piece with chilli heat and a gentle tang.

1. Prepare cucumbers: Wash thoroughly. Halve lengthways, scrape out seeds with a spoon to prevent excess wateriness, and slice into 1cm (½in) half-moons.

2. Salt: Toss cucumbers with coarse salt in a large bowl. Leave for 30 minutes, tossing halfway. Drain thoroughly but do not rinse; the light salinity helps the paste cling.

3. Make paste: In the same large bowl, combine the gochugaru, fish sauce (or kelp water), garlic, ginger, grated pear or apple, plum syrup and kelp water. Stir to a smooth, thick paste. Adjust with a splash of the reserved cucumber brine if it's too dry.

4. Mix: Add the drained cucumbers and red onions to the paste, tossing gently to coat evenly. Add garlic chives, spring onions and chilli last, gently folding through.

5. Jar and ferment: Pack into a clean jar, pressing down gently to remove air pockets but without crushing the cucumbers. Leave about 2cm (¾in) of headspace, wipe the rim and seal. Leave at room temperature for 1–2 days, tasting daily. Refrigerate once lightly tangy.

6. Storage: Refrigerate for up to 5 days, but it's best within 3 days.

Serving Suggestions

• Serve alongside grilled bulgogi, pork or fried fish.
• Pair with hot rice as a cooling, spicy contrast.
• Chop finely and stir through cold noodle salads or soba bowls.
• Scatter over avocado toast or grain bowls for a modern twist.
• Mix into potato salad for a spicy, refreshing crunch.

Goguma Mul (Purple Sweet Potato) Kimchi
고구마 물김치

Prep: 20 minutes
Brining: 10 minutes
Fermentation: 24–36 hours at room temperature before refrigeration
Makes: 3–4 litre (5¼–7 pint) jar

500g (1lb 2oz) purple sweet potato
500g (1lb 2oz) Korean radish (mu) or daikon
100g (3½oz) spring onions, cut into 2cm (¾in) pieces
2 small red chillies, halved, deseeded and thinly sliced

FOR THE BRINE

20g (¾oz) plain flour
30g (1oz) coarse sea salt
2 litres (3½ pints) water

FOR THE SPICE POUCH

1 medium pear (about 200g/7oz), grated
30g (1oz) garlic, grated
10g (⅓oz) ginger, grated

Water kimchi (mul kimchi) is the cleanest, most refreshing branch of the kimchi family. Unlike the bold, fiery spice of baechu kimchi or the deep funk of aged varieties, mul kimchi is delicate, lightly tangy, and hydrating. This version uses purple sweet potatoes as the star ingredient, and as they rest in the brine, they release anthocyanin pigments that transform the liquid into a soft lavender-pink, as if the jar itself were steeped in flowers.

This kimchi is particularly suited for those who find spicy foods difficult to digest: children, the elderly or anyone seeking a milder probiotic food. The sweet potato lends an earthy sweetness that balances the clean, fruity broth, while the daikon radish provides crunch and a slight peppery undertone. A grated pear enriches the brine, creating a subtle sweetness that ferments into complexity. This is a kimchi to serve cold on a hot day, as a soup-like side or even as a natural digestive tonic to sip between meals.

1. Prepare vegetables: Wash and peel the purple sweet potato and radish. Slice both into matchsticks about 2cm (¾in) long and 0.5 cm (¼in) thick.

2. Make brine: In a saucepan, whisk the flour and salt into the water. Bring to a gentle boil over a medium heat, whisking to remove any clumps. Simmer for 3–5 minutes until the liquid turns slightly cloudy, then remove from heat and let cool completely. This light flour brine helps flavours adhere and supports lactic fermentation.

3. Assemble the spice pouch: Grate the pear and place in a 15 × 15cm (6 × 6in) mesh bag or muslin cloth. Add the garlic and ginger. Tie securely. This pouch keeps the brine clear while infusing it with flavour.

4. Combine: In a large jar, layer the sweet potato, radish, spring onion and chilli. Pour the cooled brine over the vegetables, leaving 2cm (¾in) of headspace. Submerge the spice pouch into the liquid, ensuring it sits in the middle for even flavour distribution. Stir gently to remove air bubbles. Wipe the rim and seal.

5. Ferment: Leave the jar at room temperature (18–22°C/65–70°F) for 24–36 hours. The brine should taste lightly tangy and fragrant with pear, garlic and

ginger. The broth will begin to take on a soft lavender-pink colour as the sweet potatoes infuse.

6. Store: Remove the pouch, if you like, and refrigerate the kimchi. Burp the jar daily for the first 7 days. It will continue fermenting slowly in the fridge, keeping well for up to 2 weeks.

Serving Suggestions

- Serve chilled in small bowls with both broth and vegetables, like a refreshing soup.
- Pair with fried foods (pajeon, fried chicken, croquettes) for a cleansing balance.
- Offer as a palate cleanser between heavier courses.
- Sip the pink brine like a light tonic – it is hydrating, probiotic-rich and soothing.

Kimmy's Notes

- **Colour intensity:** Some purple sweet potatoes bleed colour more vividly than others. If the broth is pale, slice potatoes slightly thinner next time to increase pigment release.
- **Brine clarity:** Using a spice pouch keeps the broth clear. Without it, the liquid may go cloudy but will still tastes excellent.
- **Fermentation speed:** Warmer rooms may bring tang in under 24 hours; cooler kitchens may need 36 hours. Always taste before refrigerating.
- **Alternative method:** Instead of flour paste, dissolve 30g (1oz) of salt directly in 2 litres (3½ pints) of water for a lighter, clearer brine. The flour adds body but is optional.

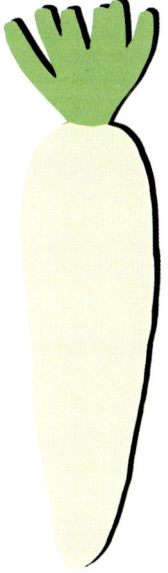

Watermelon Rind Kimchi
수박껍질 김치

Prep: 25 minutes
Brining: 30 minutes
Fermentation: 1–3 days at room temperature before refrigeration
Makes: 1 litre (1¾ pint) jar

600g (1lb 5oz) watermelon rind
30g (1oz) coarse sea salt

FOR THE SEASONING PASTE

40g (1½oz) gochugaru
1½ tbsp anchovy fish sauce, or 1½ tbsp kelp water with ½ tsp salt
30g (1oz) garlic, grated
30g (1oz) ginger, grated
2 tsp maesil-cheong (plum syrup), (optional, but recommended)
20g (¾oz) spring onion, finely sliced
10g (⅓oz) fresh mint or perilla leaves, roughly torn (optional)

Kimmy's Notes

- **Shape matters:** Matchsticks give a quick crunch, while cubes hold more juice – choose depending on texture preference.
- **Herbal lift:** Mint makes this kimchi taste almost mojito-like, while perilla adds a nutty, sesame-anise aroma.
- **Fermentation speed:** In warm kitchens, it may be ready in just 24 hours. Always taste regularly before refrigerating.

In Korea, summer often means finding ways to cool down with refreshing foods, and watermelon is the fruit of choice for many households. But instead of discarding the rind, it can be turned into a crisp and surprisingly flavourful kimchi, celebrating the idea of turning scraps into treasure. The pale rind absorbs seasoning beautifully while keeping a juicy crunchy bite, making it both resourceful and delicious. The rind's mild sweetness pairs well with chilli, garlic and ginger, while the herbs lend a cooling, aromatic lift.

1. Prep rind: Slice away the hard green skin from the watermelon rind using a knife or vegetable peeler. Trim most of the pink flesh, leaving mainly the pale white rind. Cut into 0.5 cm (¼in) matchsticks or cubes.

2. Salt: Place the rind in a large bowl. Sprinkle with the salt and toss to coat. Leave for 30 minutes, mixing once halfway. Drain well in a colander, but do not rinse.

3. Make paste: In the same large bowl, combine the gochugaru, fish sauce (or kelp water), garlic, ginger and plum syrup. Mix into a loose paste.

4. Mix: Add the drained rind to the paste. Toss until evenly coated. Mix in the sliced spring onions, and, if using mint or perilla leaves, fold them in gently at the end.

5. Ferment: Transfer the mixture into a clean jar, pressing lightly to release juices and reduce air pockets. Leave 2cm (¾in) of headspace, wipe the rim and seal. Ferment at room temperature for 1–3 days, tasting daily, and refrigerating when it tastes to your liking.

6. Store: Keep it in the fridge and burp the jar daily for the first 7 days. It will be at its best within 2 weeks.

Serving Suggestions

- Serve chilled alongside grilled meats or a summer barbecue.
- Pair with cold noodles like naengmyeon or soba.
- Add to salads for crunch and heat.
- Drink the brine as a cooling probiotic tonic on hot days.

Summer Herb Kimchi

VEGAN

Prep: 15 minutes
Brining: 15 minutes
Fermentation: 12–24 hours at room temperature
Makes: 500ml (17½fl oz) jar

300g (10½oz) mixed soft herbs, such as parsley, coriander, dill, mint, sorrel and Thai basil
1 tsp coarse sea salt
100g (3½oz) daikon, julienned
15g (½oz) spring onion, finely sliced on the diagonal (optional)

FOR THE SEASONING PASTE

10g (⅓oz) gochugaru, or to taste
10g (⅓oz) garlic, grated
10g (⅓oz) ginger, grated
1 tbsp filtered water
2 tsp coarse sea salt

Kimmy's Notes

- **Brine:** If the herbs look dry, add another 1–2 tablespoons of filtered water before sealing the jar.
- **Storage:** Keep refrigerated after day 1. Herbs will darken quickly, so enjoy while green.

A tangle of soft, fragrant leaves becomes a fleeting summer kimchi in this delicate ferment. Instead of sturdy napa cabbage or radish, this recipe celebrates herbs at their freshest: parsley, coriander, dill, mint, and even wild greens if you can find them. The leaves wilt quickly, drinking in garlic, ginger and chilli, releasing a perfumed brine that feels more like a herbal tonic than a heavy paste. This is a kimchi you enjoy young, bright-green and alive. Perfect spooned over rice, stirred through grilled vegetables, or served alongside fish and barbecues on hot days.

1. Prepare herbs: Rinse herbs well in cold water to remove any grit. Dry thoroughly in a salad spinner or between clean towels. Remove any tough stems and gently tear large leaves.

2. Salt: Place herbs in a large bowl. Sprinkle with the salt, toss lightly and leave for 15 minutes to wilt. Drain gently in a colander without rinsing.

3. Make paste: In the same large bowl, mix the gochugaru, garlic, ginger, water and the remaining salt into a spreadable paste.

4. Combine: Wearing gloves, gently toss herbs and vegetables with the paste, coating everything evenly but carefully to avoid bruising the herbs.

5. Pack into jar: Transfer the mixture into a clean jar. Press down lightly to remove air pockets but avoid crushing the leaves. Leave about 2cm (¾in) of headspace, wipe the rim and seal.

6. Ferment: Leave at room temperature (18–22°C/65–70°F) for 12–24 hours. Once brine develops and the herbs taste lightly sour, refrigerate to slow fermentation.

7. Store: Keep in the fridge and enjoy within 3–4 days while the herbs are still bright.

Serving Suggestions

- Scatter over freshly steamed rice or quinoa.
- Toss with boiled new potatoes for a summer salad.
- Add as a garnish for grilled fish or chicken.
- Stir into cold noodle dishes for fragrance and crunch.

Cherry Tomato Kimchi

VEGAN

Prep: 20 minutes
Brining: 30 minutes
Fermentation: 1–2 days at room temperature before refrigeration
Makes: 500ml (17½fl oz) jar

300g (10½oz) cherry tomatoes
20g (¾oz) coarse sea salt
15 fresh basil leaves (or perilla leaves for a Korean twist)

FOR THE SEASONING PASTE

15g (½oz) gochugaru, or to taste
10g (⅓oz) garlic, grated
10g (⅓oz) ginger, grated
1 tbsp filtered water

Kimmy's Notes

- **Tomato choice:** Use firm cherry or grape tomatoes. Avoid overripe ones – they collapse quickly.
- **Speedy ferment:** In hot kitchens, they may be fizzy in just 12–18 hours, so taste sooner.
- **Brine bonus:** Don't discard the liquid. It's tangy, slightly sweet and perfect as a mixer or dressing base.

Cherry tomatoes may not seem like traditional kimchi material, but once salted and seasoned, they transform into little flavour-packed jewels. Their skins firm up, the flesh softens, and when you bite into one, it releases a sweet, tangy, spicy burst of juice. Unlike cabbage or radish kimchi, this version is best enjoyed young..

In Korea, tomato kimchi is a modern seasonal experiment rather than an old tradition, but it perfectly captures the spirit of summer – quick ferments, light acidity and vibrant freshness. The brine itself becomes a bonus: effervescent, slightly sweet and drinkable on its own or stirred into sparkling water or cocktails.

1. Prep tomatoes: Rinse and dry the tomatoes well. Use a toothpick or skewer to prick each tomato once to help the seasoning penetrate and to prevent bursting during the fermentation.

2. Salt: Place tomatoes in a bowl and toss with the coarse salt. Leave for 30 minutes, tossing once midway, until they release a little liquid.

3. Make paste: In a small bowl, mix the gochugaru, garlic, ginger and filtered water to form a smooth paste.

4. Mix: Drain the salted tomatoes, but don't rinse them. Toss them into the bowl with the paste, add the basil leaves and mix gently until evenly coated.

5. Ferment: Pack into a clean jar, pressing lightly to remove air but keeping the tomatoes whole. Leave 2cm (¾in) of headspace, wipe the rim and seal. Leave to ferment at room temperature (18–22°C/65–70°F) for 1–2 days. Once lightly fizzy, transfer to the fridge.

6. Store: Burp the jar daily. They are best between days 3–5. After 1 week they will lose their texture but get deeper in flavour.

Serving Suggestions

- Pair with grilled chicken or pork at a barbecue.
- Scatter over burrata or mozzarella with olive oil for a Korean-Italian twist.
- Stir brine into a Bloody Mary or sparkling water for a probiotic kick.
- Mix with fresh herbs and toss through cold pasta or couscous salad.

Nectarine & Kohlrabi White Kimchi

VEGAN

Prep: 20–25 minutes
Brining: 30–40 minutes
Fermentation: 1–2 days at room temperature before refrigeration
Makes: 1 litre (1¾ pint) jar

300g (10½oz) kohlrabi, peeled and cut into matchsticks
200g (7oz) firm nectarines, thinly sliced
20g (¾oz) coarse sea salt
450ml (15¾fl oz) cold filtered water

FOR THE SEASONING PASTE

10g (⅓oz) garlic, grated
10g (⅓oz) ginger, grated
5g (⅛oz) fresh chives, finely chopped (optional)
20g (¾oz) pear, finely minced (for sweetness, optional)

Kimmy's Notes

• **Fruit choice:** Use firm nectarines or peaches; overripe fruit will collapse too quickly. Or try crisp apples or firm pears when stone fruit isn't in season.
• **Brine:** The liquid becomes a delicate, drinkable broth, so don't throw it away.

This gentle summer kimchi balances the crispness of kohlrabi with the floral sweetness of ripe nectarines. Unlike fiery red kimchi, this white kimchi is mild, refreshing and fruit-forward. The pale broth develops a light tang that feels almost floral, making it as much a drink as a pickle. Best enjoyed young, it's a cooling side dish that pairs beautifully with grilled meats, seafood or simply a bowl of steamed rice.

1. Prep fruit and veg: Peel kohlrabi and cut into matchsticks. Slice nectarines thinly, keeping the skin for colour.

2. Brine: Place the kohlrabi and nectarine in a bowl. Sprinkle with the salt and pour over the water. Toss, then leave for 30–40 minutes until lightly softened. Drain the kohlrabi and nectarine over a bowl, reserving the brine.

3. Make paste: In the same bowl, mix the garlic, ginger and chives and/or pear, if using.

4. Combine: Add the kohlrabi and nectarine into the bowl with the paste. Wearing gloves, gently mix with the paste until evenly coated.

5. Pack jar: Transfer to a clean jar. Pour over enough reserved brine just to cover, leaving 2cm (¾in) of headspace. Wipe the rim and seal.

6. Ferment: Ferment at room temperature for 1–2 days, checking the flavour, then refrigerate.

7. Store: Burp the jar daily for the first 7 days. Best enjoyed within 7–10 days when the flavour has deepened and before the fruit softens too much.

Serving Suggestions

• Serve chilled as a cooling side dish on hot days.
• Ladle kimchi broth into small bowls as a refreshing sip.
• Pair with grilled mackerel, salmon or pork belly.
• Slice and scatter over green salads for sweet-sour crunch.

Cucumber & Mint Kimchi

Prep: 20 minutes
Brining: 30 minutes
Fermentation: 1–2 days at room temperature before refrigeration
Makes: 1 litre (1¾ pint) jar

800g (1lb 12oz) Korean cucumbers (or firm mini/Persian cucumbers)
30g (1oz) coarse sea salt
15g (½oz) spring onions, sliced into 2cm (¾in) lengths
15g (½oz) fresh mint leaves, roughly torn

FOR THE SEASONING PASTE

40g (1½oz) gochugaru
2 tbsp anchovy fish sauce, or 2 tbsp kelp water with ½ tsp salt
20g (¾oz) garlic, grated
10g (⅓oz) ginger, grated

Serving Suggestions

• Eat straight from the jar as a refreshing summer snack.
• Serve with barbecued meats or grilled fish for a cooling contrast.
• Spoon over plain rice with sesame oil for a simple meal.

Kimmy's Notes

• Korean, Persian or mini cucumbers are best; English can be used if halved lengthways, deseeded and sliced into 1cm (½in) half-moons. They soften quickly so make a small batch and eat it fresh.
• If too salty, rinse cucumbers briefly after draining (this will slightly slow fermentation).
• This can sour within 12–18 hours, so keep an eye on it.

Crisp, juicy and cooling, this kimchi is the taste of summer in a jar. Cucumbers naturally hold a high water content, which makes them quick to ferment and perfect for warm weather when heavier ferments can feel overwhelming. The addition of fresh mint gives a cooling lift, while gochugaru provides a vibrant chilli warmth. This recipe is designed to be enjoyed young – at its peak when still fizzy, bright and crunchy. Think of it as a reset dish: light enough to eat as a snack straight from the jar, but versatile enough to serve alongside grilled meats, rice bowls or even folded into a salad.

1. Prepare cucumbers: Wash the cucumbers well, cut lengthways and scoop out the watery seeds with a spoon. Slice into half-moons about 1cm (½in) thick. This prevents the kimchi from becoming too watery.

2. Salt: Place cucumber slices in a large bowl. Sprinkle with the salt and toss evenly. Leave for 30 minutes, mixing once halfway to draw out the water. Drain thoroughly in a colander but do not rinse; the surface salt helps fermentation.

3. Make paste: In the same large bowl, mix the gochugaru, fish sauce (or kelp water), garlic and ginger. Adjust consistency with 1–2 teaspoons of water if too thick. The paste should coat the cucumbers without clumping.

4. Combine: Add the drained cucumbers to the seasoning paste and, wearing gloves, toss gently until coated. Finally, fold in the spring onions and mint, mixing lightly to avoid bruising the herbs.

5. Pack jar: Transfer the mixture into a clean jar. Press down lightly to remove air pockets, but don't crush the cucumbers. Leave about 2cm (¾in) of headspace, wipe the rim and seal.

6. Ferment: Leave at room temperature for 1–2 days, depending on ambient temperature. Taste daily. When bubbles start rising and the flavour is tangy but still fresh, transfer to the fridge.

7. Store: Burp the jar daily, and eat within 5–7 days for maximum crunch and bright mint aroma. Longer storage will lead to softer cucumbers and stronger sourness.

Courgette Ribbon Kimchi

VEGAN

Prep time: 15 minutes
Brining: 20 minutes
Fermentation: 12–24 hours at room temperature before refrigeration
Makes: 500ml (17½fl oz) jar

300g (10½oz) courgettes (about 2 small, firm courgettes)
10g (⅓oz) coarse sea salt

FOR THE SEASONING PASTE

10g (⅓oz) gochugaru
10g (⅓oz) garlic, grated
10g (⅓oz) ginger, grated
1 tbsp filtered water
10g (⅓oz) fresh dill (or chives, mint or parsley), finely chopped (optional)
Zest of ½ lemon (for brightness, optional)

Serving Suggestions

- Serve alongside grilled fish, halloumi or chicken skewers.
- Toss with cold soba noodles for a cooling summer meal.
- Pair with soft cheeses like ricotta or mozzarella for a light appetiser.
- Use as a quick taco or wrap filling with beans and herbs.

Kimmy's Notes

- **Courgette:** Smaller, firm courgettes make the best ribbons – larger can be watery.
- **Brine bonus:** Don't discard the liquid. It's tangy, slightly sweet and perfect as a mixer or dressing base.

Courgette ribbon kimchi is one of the most delicate you can make – light and almost salad-like. Thin ribbons of courgette soak up the flavours of the seasonings, becoming silky yet refreshing, with a whisper of chilli. This kind of kimchi is best eaten within a day or two while the ribbons still hold their freshness and tender bite. It looks beautiful on the table, its green curls catch the light and its taste is subtle enough to pair with grilled fish, fresh cheeses or even tucked into sandwiches. In Korea, quick greens like courgette (a modern substitute for summer squash varieties) are often seasoned lightly and enjoyed the same day. This kimchi follows that spirit – closer to a fresh banchan than a long-aged ferment.

1. Prepare courgette: Rinse and dry the courgettes. Using a vegetable peeler or mandolin, slice lengthways into thin ribbons, turning the courgette as you go. Stop when you reach the seedy core (set aside for stir-fries or soups). The goal is soft, even ribbons without watery seeds.

2. Salt: Place the ribbons in a large mixing bowl and sprinkle with 10g (⅓oz) sea salt. Toss gently, ensuring the salt touches every strand. Leave for 20 minutes until softened and slightly wilted. Drain in a colander, pressing lightly to release excess water. Do not rinse.

3. Make paste: In the same bowl, combine the gochugaru, garlic, ginger and filtered water. Mix into a smooth paste. If using dill or lemon zest, stir them in now for an aromatic lift.

4. Mix: Wearing gloves, toss the drained ribbons gently with the paste until evenly coated. Handle them delicately so the ribbons remain intact.

5. Pack: Place the ribbons loosely into a clean jar, pressing lightly but not too firmly (you don't want a compact block). Leave about 2cm (¾in) of headspace, wipe the rim and seal.

6. Ferment: Leave at room temperature for 12–24 hours. Check after 12 hours – if you like it lightly sour with a salad-like crunch, refrigerate immediately. For a touch more tang, let sit for up to 24 hours before refrigerating.

7. Store: It is best eaten within 1–2 days; after 3 days it will start to lose its texture.

AUTUMN – ABUNDANT, ROBUST & SHAREABLE

Autumn is the season of grounding. After summer's brightness, the air cools, days shorten and our bodies crave foods that are deeper and more sustaining. In Korea, this marks the turn towards winter, when families prepare larger batches of kimchi to carry them through the cold months.

Markets shift too. Cucumbers and tender greens give way to sturdy roots, squashes and dark cabbages. These ingredients bring earthy strength, perfect for ferments that feel generous and nourishing. Autumn jars are not as fleeting as in the warmer months, but lingering, designed to be eaten slowly, their flavours evolving over weeks.

Roots like sweet potato, carrot and beetroot provide natural sweetness, softening the acidity of fermentation. Brassicas such as kale and Savoy cabbage add minerality and backbone. Fruits – especially pear, a traditional Korean addition – brighten the mix and help fermentation along. In this section you'll find recipes that are hearty and sustaining, meant for sharing in the centre of the table as the evenings draw in.

Beetroot & Pear Kimchi

VEGAN

Prep: 20 minutes
Brining: 30–40 minutes
Fermentation: 2–3 days at room temperature before refrigeration
Makes: 750ml (1 pint 5fl oz) jar

200g (7oz) raw beetroot, peeled and thinly sliced or julienned
200g (7oz) pear (ripe, but firm), thinly sliced
15g (½oz) coarse sea salt
100ml (3½fl oz) filtered water

FOR THE SEASONING PASTE

1 tsp gochugaru
2 garlic cloves, grated
2.5cm (1in) ginger, grated
3 thyme sprigs, leaves only, or fennel fronds, roughly chopped (optional)

Serving Suggestions

- With goat cheese or soft cheeses on toast.
- Alongside roast meats or baked squash.
- Tossed into salads with bitter greens.
- As part of a cheese or charcuterie board.

Kimmy's Notes

- **Variation**: Add a few slices of red onion for sharpness and extra crunch.
- **Colour**: Beetroot stains everything – including your hands – so gloves are helpful.
- **Gifting**: This kimchi makes a stunning homemade gift; pack it into a jar with a ribbon once fermentation settles.

This kimchi is a celebration of contrasts: the deep, iron-rich earthiness of beetroot against the fragrant sweetness of ripe pear. Where traditional kimchi often leans on Asian pear to balance spice and salt, here the fruit takes centre stage, softening and sweetening the intensity of beetroot. The result is a ferment that looks as striking as it tastes – stained a jewel-like crimson, slightly floral, and naturally sweet without added sugar. Using firm Conference or Comice pears ensures they hold their shape through fermentation, while the beetroot releases its colour and develops tangy, jammy notes over time. Within a few days the kimchi is mild and fruity, but after a week it becomes more complex, elegant and layered. This is a kimchi that feels at home both on a Korean table and on a European cheese board.

1. Salt vegetables: Place the beetroot and pear in a large mixing bowl. Sprinkle with salt and pour over filtered water. Toss well to coat and leave for 30–40 minutes, tossing once or twice, until slightly softened. Drain the beetroot and pear, reserving the brine.

2. Prepare seasoning paste: In the same large bowl, combine gochugaru, garlic, ginger and gradually stir in the reserved brine until you have a light slurry. Add in the herbs, if using.

3. Mix: Add the vegetables to the paste and, wearing gloves, mix thoroughly until everything is evenly coated.

4. Pack into jar: Transfer the mixture to a clean jar, pressing down firmly to remove air pockets. Pour over any leftover paste and enough reserved brine to just cover, leaving 2cm (¾in) of headspace. Wipe the rim and seal.

5. Ferment and store: Ferment at room temperature (18–22°C/65–70°F) for 2–3 days, checking daily. Once tangy and lightly floral, tighten the lid and refrigerate. Burp the jar daily for the first 7 days. Flavours will deepen over the next week, becoming richer and slightly jammy, and the pear will soften. It is best eaten within 1–2 weeks.

Kale & Sweet Potato Kimchi

VEGAN

Prep: 30-40 minutes
Brining: 30-60 minutes
Fermentation: 2-4 days at room temperature before refrigeration
Makes: 750ml (1 pint 5fl oz) jar

400g (14oz) sweet potato, peeled, cut into 1-2cm (½-¾in) cubes
200g (7oz) curly kale, thick stalks removed, leaves torn into bite-size pieces
2 tbsp coarse sea salt (about 30g/1oz)

FOR THE SEASONING PASTE

35-40g (1¼oz) gochugaru, to taste
25g (1oz) garlic, grated
20g (¾oz) ginger, grated
3 spring onions, thinly sliced
50g (1¾oz) Asian pear or apple, grated, or 1 tbsp pear or apple juice
1-2 tsp filtered water, as needed, to loosen paste

Kimmy's Notes

- **Sweet potato type:** Use firm, waxy varieties – they keep their structure better than floury ones, which can become mushy.
- **Kale substitute:** Cavolo nero works well for a darker, more robust version. Spinach or chard can also be used, but the fermentation will be shorter.
- **Fermentation speed:** In warmer climates, begin tasting on day 2. In cooler kitchens, fermentation may take 4-5 days.

This kimchi is a celebration of autumn's shift in mood and flavour. Kale and sweet potatoes are two ingredients that thrive in the cooler months, and together they create a kimchi that feels both grounding and nourishing. The sweetness of raw sweet potato balances the grassy depth of kale, while the seasoning paste of garlic, ginger and gochugaru brings warmth. This kimchi has a distinctly chewy texture: the sweet potato softens but never loses its bite, while kale transforms from tough and fibrous into tender, tangy ribbons during fermentation.

The character of this kimchi evolves as it ages. In the first few days it tastes clean, almost salad-like, with a bright, vegetal edge. After a week, the flavours settle into harmony: sweet, savoury, slightly tart. By 2 to 3 weeks, it becomes more robust – sour, earthy and deeply satisfying, perfect alongside roasted meats or spooned onto warm rice. I think of this as an 'evening kimchi', one to bring out when the nights get longer, the windows fog with steam and the table calls for something hearty.

1. Salt vegetables: Place the cubed sweet potato and kale leaves in a large mixing bowl. Sprinkle over the sea salt and massage gently with your hands for 2-3 minutes. The kale will darken and soften slightly, releasing water. Leave for 30-60 minutes, tossing once or twice.

2. Make paste: In a separate bowl, combine the gochugaru, garlic, ginger, spring onions and the grated pear or apple or juice. Mix into a thick, fragrant paste. If it feels too stiff, add the filtered water. The paste should be spreadable but not watery.

3. Mix: Drain away any liquid that has collected in the salted vegetables (do not rinse). Wearing gloves, add the seasoning paste to the bowl and massage into the kale and sweet potato until every piece is thoroughly coated. Taste a piece and adjust, if needed – more gochugaru for heat, or a splash more apple or pear juice for sweetness.

4. Pack jar: Transfer the mixture into a clean jar, pressing down firmly to release the natural juices and remove air pockets. Leave about 2cm (¾in) of headspace at the top to allow gases to escape. Wipe the rim and seal with a loose lid or fermentation cap.

5. Ferment: Leave the jar at room temperature for 2–4 days, depending on the warmth of your kitchen. Taste daily after day 2. When it has reached your preferred balance of crunch and sourness, move it to the fridge to slow fermentation. The flavour will continue to mature over the following weeks.

6. Store: Burp the jar daily for the first 7 days. It will keep in the fridge for 6–8 weeks, with the flavour intensifying over time.

Serving Suggestions

- Serve with steamed brown rice and roasted seasonal vegetables.
- Pairs beautifully with grilled halloumi, roast chicken or pork belly.
- Add a spoonful to grain bowls or autumn soups for brightness.
- Chop and fold into warm lentils or quinoa for a nourishing, plant-based meal.

Carrot, Ginger & Pear Kimchi

VEGAN

Prep: 15 minutes
Brining: 20–30 minutes
Fermentation: 1–2 days at room temperature before refrigeration
Makes: 500ml (17½fl oz) jar

200g (7oz) carrots, thinly sliced into rectangular pieces
100g (3½oz) pear (ripe, but firm), cut into rectangular pieces
100g (3½oz) ginger, peeled and thinly cut into rectangular pieces
15g (½oz) coarse sea salt
50ml (1¾fl oz) filtered water

FOR THE SEASONING PASTE

30g (1oz) gochugaru
1 garlic clove, grated
15g (½oz) ginger, grated

Kimmy's Notes

- **Texture:** Julienne carrots for extra crunch, grate them for softer texture.
- **Balance:** If it gets too sharp, stir through an extra spoonful of grated pear just before serving.

This kimchi is sunshine in a jar – crisp carrots paired with the warming heat of ginger and the natural sweetness of ripe pear. It's a short, bright ferment that brings energy to your table, ready in just a couple of days. The pear speeds fermentation while adding balance, and the ginger gives a lively kick that makes this kimchi especially refreshing in autumn. You can keep it mild by leaving out the gochugaru.

1. Salt vegetables: Place the carrots and pear in a large bowl. Add the salt and filtered water, tossing well to coat. Leave for 20–30 minutes until the carrots soften slightly. Drain, reserving the brine. Do not rinse.

2. Make paste: In the same bowl, combine the gochugaru, garlic and ginger. Add 1–2 teaspoons of the reserved brine if the paste feels too stiff.

3. Mix and coat: Add the drained carrots and pear to the paste. Wearing gloves, massage gently until every piece is evenly coated.

4. Pack jar: Transfer the mixture into a clean jar, pressing down firmly to remove air pockets. Pour in any leftover paste or liquid leaving 2cm (¾in) of headspace. Wipe the rim and seal.

5. Ferment: Ferment at room temperature (18–22°C/65–70°F) for 1–2 days, tasting daily. When tangy and bright, tighten the lid and refrigerate.

6. Store: Burp the jar daily, and enjoy within 1 week while still crunchy.

Serving Suggestions

- With bibimbap or grain bowls for colour and crunch.
- In wraps or sandwiches to add brightness.
- Tossed into cold noodle dishes for a refreshing kick.
- Stirred into hummus or served on flatbreads.
- Alongside creamy cheeses, roast meats or autumn salads.

Pumpkin & Sage Kimchi

VEGAN

Prep: 20 minutes
Brining: 30 minutes
Fermentation: 2–3 days at room temperature before refrigeration
Makes: 750ml (1 pint 5fl oz) jar

300g (10½oz) pumpkin or winter squash, peeled and cubed into 2–3 cm (1in) pieces
15g (½oz) coarse sea salt
5 sage leaves, finely chopped
2 tbsp filtered water

FOR THE SEASONING PASTE

20g (¾oz) gochugaru
15g (½oz) garlic, grated
10g (⅓oz) ginger, grated
15g (½oz) spring onion, finely chopped
30g (1oz) Asian pear or apple, grated
2 tbsp filtered water

Serving Suggestions

- Warm with cooked lentils or grains for a hearty side.
- Blend into a purée to serve under fish.
- Use as a topping for sourdough, sprinkled with nuts and seeds.
- Stir through risottos or pasta or add some to soups for an autumnal twist.

Kimmy's Notes

- **Pumpkin choice:** Firm-fleshed varieties like kabocha or crown prince squash hold their shape best. Avoid watery pumpkins, which ferment unevenly.

This kimchi is autumn in a jar – cosy, fragrant and quietly sophisticated. Pumpkin may not be a traditional Korean ingredient, but its natural sweetness, dense texture and mellow flavour lends itself beautifully to fermentation. Steaming the cubes briefly before seasoning helps soften their edges without losing bite, creating a kimchi that feels soft yet structured. Sage brings something unexpected here: a resinous, slightly bitter depth that counteracts pumpkin's gentle sweetness. Together they form a pairing that is both familiar to European kitchens and in harmony with the Korean fermentation tradition.

1. Steam pumpkin: Place the pumpkin or squash in a steamer over a pan of barely simmering water. Steam lightly for 3–4 minutes, until the cubes begin to soften at the edges but remain firm in the centre. Set aside and allow to cool completely.

2. Brine: Place the cooled pumpkin in a large bowl. Toss with the sea salt, chopped sage and filtered water. Leave for 30 minutes, tossing occasionally, until the pumpkin begins to release a little liquid. Drain gently if needed, but avoid rinsing.

3. Make paste: In a small bowl, mix the gochugaru, garlic, ginger, spring onion, grated pear and water. Stir to form a smooth paste.

4. Mix: Add the paste to the salted pumpkin. Wearing gloves, gently mix until all cubes are evenly coated without breaking them apart.

5. Pack jar: Transfer the seasoned pumpkin into a clean jar, pressing down lightly to remove air pockets. Spoon in any remaining paste or liquid, leaving 2cm (¾in) of headspace at the top. Wipe the rim and seal.

6. Ferment: Leave at room temperature (18–22°C/65–70°F) for 2–3 days, checking daily. When a light tang develops, transfer to the fridge.

7. Store: For the best depth of flavour, allow the kimchi to mature for 5–7 days (burping the jar daily) before eating, by which time the pumpkin has absorbed the flavours of garlic, ginger and chilli while releasing just enough of its own sugars to deepen the ferment. It is best enjoyed within 2 weeks before it softens fully.

Savoy Cabbage Kimchi

VEGAN

Prep: 20 minutes
Brining: 1–2 hours
Fermentation: 2–3 days at room temperature
Makes: 750ml (1 pint 5fl oz) jar

Savoy cabbage, chopped into bite-size pieces, about 3 × 3cm (1 × 1in)
200g (7oz) daikon, chopped into bite-size pieces
30g (1oz) coarse sea salt
240ml (8½fl oz) filtered water

FOR THE SEASONING PASTE

30g (1oz) gochugaru
30g (1oz) garlic, grated
30g (1oz) ginger, grated
15g (½oz) spring onion, chopped
1 tbsp filtered water

Serving Suggestions

- With roast meats, sausages or baked squash.
- Stirred into soups or mashed potatoes.
- Layered on rye or sourdough bread.

Kimmy's Notes

- **Brining:** Don't oversalt Savoy – it softens quickly and doesn't need heavy brining.
- **Balance:** For additional sweetness, add a spoonful of grated pear or a splash of apple juice to the paste.

Savoy cabbage is not a traditional Korean ingredient, but it makes a beautiful seasonal kimchi, especially in autumn. Its pale green, crinkled leaves soften just enough in the brine while still holding their shape, and their nutty, buttery flavour pairs wonderfully with the chilli, garlic and ginger of classic kimchi seasoning.

Unlike baechu (napa cabbage), Savoy's leaves have ridges that grip the seasoning paste, giving each bite extra depth and texture. You can treat it just like standard kimchi with a salt, season and ferment, or even roll the leaves into bundles for a more elegant presentation. The result is a cool-weather kimchi that feels familiar yet slightly European, making it an excellent bridge between cultures and kitchens.

1. Salt cabbage: Place the chopped cabbage and daikon in a large mixing bowl. Dissolve the sea salt in the filtered water and pour over the vegetables. Weigh down with a plate or jar so the leaves stay submerged. Leave for 1–2 hours until softened.

2. Drain and rinse: Drain the vegetables in a colander, then rinse gently with cold water to remove excess salt. Shake off the water and set aside.

3. Make paste: In the same bowl, mix together the gochugaru, garlic, ginger, spring onion, daikon and filtered water to form a paste.

4. Mix: Return the cabbage to the bowl with the seasoning paste. Wearing gloves, gently massage the seasoning paste into the drained cabbage until it's evenly coated.

5. Pack jar: Transfer the veg into a clean jar. Press down firmly to remove air pockets, and pour in any leftover paste or liquid, leaving 2cm (¾in) of headspace at the top. Wipe the rim and seal.

6. Ferment: Ferment at room temperature (18–22°C/ 65–70°F) for 2–3 days, tasting daily. When tangy and aromatic, tighten the lid and refrigerate.

7. Store: Burp the jar daily for the first 7 days. It is best enjoyed within 1–2 weeks, as the leaves soften and deepen in flavour.

WINTER – DEEP, SLOW & COMFORTING

In Korea, winter is a season of pause and preparation. Days grow short, the ground hardens and life slows its rhythm. Vegetables respond by thickening their leaves, deepening their roots and concentrating their flavours. Kimchi follows the same pattern. If spring is renewal and summer is immediacy, then winter is patience. Ferments are never rushed; they sit quietly, the cold air slowing transformation to a measured crawl.

This is the moment of kimjang. Families gathering to salt mountains of cabbage, trim radishes and stir great bowls of paste before filling onggi and, historically, burying them in the ground. The earth itself became refrigerator and shield, keeping kimchi just above freezing so it could ferment steadily all winter.

Winter kimchi is deeper and heartier than the quick styles of summer. Brassicas, roots and sturdy greens – such as Brussels sprouts, leeks, celeriac, parsnips, swede and turnips – withstand long, slow fermentation and emerge bold yet balanced. At the table, they stand alongside stews, braises and roasts, transforming winter food into something sustaining and alive.

Parsnip Kimchi

Prep: 20 minutes
Brining: 30 minutes
Fermentation: 2–4 days at room temperature, before refrigeration
Makes: 1 litre (1¾ pint) jar

500g (1lb 2oz) parsnips
20g (¾oz) coarse sea salt

FOR THE SEASONING PASTE

30g (1oz) gochugaru
1½ tbsp anchovy fish sauce, or 1½ tbsp kelp water with ½ tsp salt
15g (½oz) garlic, grated
10g (⅓oz) ginger, grated
15g (½oz) spring onions, finely sliced

Serving Suggestions

- Perfect with roasted meats or root vegetables.
- Lovely alongside nutty grains like barley or farro.
- Works as a unique addition to cheese platters or sandwiches.
- Mixed into mashed potatoes for a fiery, sweet twist on a classic side.

Kimmy's Notes

- **Flavour balance:** Parsnips are naturally sweet – don't skimp on the chilli to keep flavours lively.
- **Texture:** Softer than celeriac or radish kimchi, parsnip kimchi is best eaten within the first week.

Parsnips are rarely thought of as a kimchi base, but their natural sweetness and creamy, starchy texture make them a delightful surprise. In fermentation, parsnips take on a dual character: they remain sweet and nutty at the core, while the chilli, garlic and ginger paste wraps them in spice and savoury depth.

This kimchi is perfect for the colder months, when parsnips are in season and their sugars are at their peak. Unlike radish or celeriac, parsnips soften more quickly, producing a kimchi that is less about sharp crunch and more about a balance of tender bite and layered flavour. The sweet-spicy contrast makes it especially good alongside roasts, where it cuts through rich meats or hearty vegetarian mains. After a few days, the kimchi develops a mellow heat and a gentle tang that complements its natural sweetness beautifully.

1. Prepare the parsnips: Peel the parsnips and cut into thin batons, similar to fries or matchsticks. This size allows them to absorb seasoning evenly.

2. Salt: Place in a large bowl, sprinkle with the salt and toss well. Leave for 30 minutes until lightly softened. Drain in a colander, but do not rinse.

3. Make paste: In the same large bowl, combine the gochugaru, fish sauce (or kelp water), garlic, ginger and spring onions to form a vibrant red paste.

4. Mix: Add the drained parsnips to the paste. Wearing gloves, massage gently to coat the parsnip fully.

5. Pack jar: Transfer to a clean jar, pressing down to eliminate air pockets. Leave 2cm (¾in) of headspace. Wipe the rim and seal.

6. Ferment: Leave at room temperature (18–22°C/65–70°F) for 2–4 days. Taste daily and refrigerate once tangy.

7. Store: Burp the jar daily for the first 7 days. Keep in the fridge and eat within 1–2 weeks before it gets too soft.

Celeriac Kimchi

Prep: 20 minutes
Brining: 30 minutes
Fermentation: 2-4 days at room temperature before refrigeration
Makes: 1 litre (1¾ pint) jar

600g (1lb 5oz) celeriac
20g (¾oz) coarse sea salt

FOR THE SEASONING PASTE

35g (1¼oz) gochugaru
1½ tbsp anchovy fish sauce, or 1½ tbsp kelp water with ½ tsp salt
15g (½oz) garlic, grated
10g (⅓oz) ginger, grated
15g (½oz) spring onion, sliced into 2cm (¾in) lengths

Serving Suggestions

- Paired with hearty winter stews or braised meats.
- On a charcuterie or cheese board for a tangy counterpoint.
- Add to sandwiches or grain bowls for crunch and spice.
- Mix with roasted nuts and grains for a winter salad that feels hearty yet fresh

Kimmy's Notes

- **Texture:** Celeriac holds its firmness even after fermentation, making it one of the crunchiest winter kimchi options.
- **Balance:** If the flavour is too strong, add 1 teaspoon of grated pear or apple to the paste for more natural sweetness.

Celeriac – often overlooked in favour of its cousin, celery – makes an exceptional winter kimchi ingredient. Beneath its gnarly exterior lies crisp, ivory flesh with a clean, earthy flavour and a hint of celery brightness. When fermented, celeriac transforms into something lively and fragrant: crunchy like radish, yet with its own unique perfume that carries through every bite.

This kimchi is especially rewarding in colder months when fresh, vibrant vegetables are scarce. The celeriac matchsticks stay firm during fermentation while absorbing the spicy-savoury paste. Their earthy quality balances beautifully with garlic, ginger and chilli heat. The result is a kimchi that feels sharp, refreshing and deeply aromatic – a jar that lifts heavy winter meals and pairs beautifully with rich dishes like stews, braises or charcuterie boards.

1. Prepare celeriac: Peel the celeriac thoroughly. Slice into thin batons or matchsticks for even salting and a consistent crunch.

2. Brine: Place the celeriac batons in a large bowl, sprinkle with the salt and toss well. Leave for 30 minutes, tossing once or twice, until the pieces have softened slightly and begun to release liquid. Drain in a colander but do not rinse.

3. Make paste: In the same large bowl, mix the gochugaru, fish sauce (or kelp water), garlic, ginger and spring onion until combined into a thick, red paste.

4. Mix: Add the drained celeriac to the paste and, wearing gloves, massage until all pieces are evenly coated.

5. Pack jar: Transfer into a clean jar, pressing down firmly to remove air pockets. Leave about 2cm (¾in) of headspace at the top. Wipe the rim and seal.

6. Ferment: Leave at room temperature (18–22°C/65–70°F) for 2-4 days. Taste daily and when it's tangy and aromatic, tighten the lid and refrigerate.

7. Store: Burp the jar daily for the first 7 days. Best enjoyed within 2 weeks for peak crunch.

Brussels Sprout Kimchi (Sobagi-style)

Prep: 30 minutes
Brining: 1 hour
Fermentation: 2–4 days at room temperature, before refrigeration
Makes: 1 litre (1¾ pint) jar

600g (1lb 5oz) Brussels sprouts
30g (1oz) coarse sea salt
4 tbsp filtered water

FOR THE SEASONING PASTE

50g (1¾oz) gochugaru
2 tbsp anchovy fish sauce, or 2 tbsp kelp water with ½ tsp salt
30g (1oz) garlic, grated
30g (1oz) ginger, grated
200g (7oz) daikon, julienned

Serving Suggestions

• Served with roasted meats.
• Alongside with nutty grains like farro, bulgur wheat or wild rice.
• On a cheese board, especially with sharp Cheddars or creamy blue cheeses.
• Tucked into sandwiches for heat and crunch.

Kimmy's Notes

• **Texture:** Brussels sprouts stay firmer than napa cabbage, so this kimchi has more bite. To soften further, extend the salting by 15 minutes.
• **Balance:** If the sprouts taste too bitter early on, let them ferment a little longer – the sourness will mellow the bitterness.
• **Presentation:** The sobagi-style makes this kimchi especially elegant for serving whole at the table

Brussels sprouts might not be a traditional Korean vegetable, but their dense, nutty flavour makes excellent kimchi. In this sobagi-style version, each sprout is carefully quartered but kept intact and stuffed with a spicy, aromatic paste. The result is miniature bundles of flavour – fiery on the outside, tender and juicy within. The sprouts' natural bitterness mellows during fermentation, leaving behind a deep, savoury flavour that pairs beautifully with the sharpness of garlic, the warmth of ginger and the spice of chilli. This kimchi works well as an autumn or winter ferment, when sprouts are in peak season.

1. Prepare sprouts: Wash the Brussels sprouts and trim any tough outer leaves. Standing each sprout on its base, cut a deep cross not quite fully through the sprout, leaving 0.5cm (¼in) at the stem end intact. Then score a shallow cross in the base of each half. This helps them soften during brining and creates space for the paste.

2. Salt sprouts: Place the sprouts in a large mixing bowl and sprinkle with the salt. Toss thoroughly, then add just enough of the water to help the salt cling. Leave for 1 hour, tossing occasionally, until the sprouts soften slightly and begin to release liquid. Drain in a colander, reserving the brine, but do not rinse.

3. Make paste: In the same large bowl, combine the gochugaru, fish sauce (or kelp water), garlic, ginger and julienned daikon. Mix into a thick paste. Adjust consistency with 1–2 teaspoons of the brine if too dry.

4. Stuff the sprouts: Wearing gloves, gently pry open each sprout and tuck in a small spoonful of paste. Take care not to split the leaves apart completely – the goal is to keep them intact while evenly seasoning.

5. Pack jar: Transfer into a clean jar, pressing them down to remove air. Spoon any remaining paste or liquid over the sprouts, leaving 2cm (¾in) of headspace at the top. Wipe the rim and seal.

6. Ferment: Leave at room temperature (18–22°C/65–70°F) for 2–4 days. Bubbles will start to form and the sprouts will deepen in flavour. Taste daily and when tangy and pleasantly robust, tighten the lid and refrigerate. They are best consumed within 2–3 weeks.

7. Store: Burp the jar daily for the first 7 days.

Leek & Mustard Seed Kimchi

VEGAN

Prep: 25 minutes
Brining: 30 minutes
Fermentation: 1–3 days at room temperature, before refrigeration
Makes: 1 litre (1¾ pint) jar

500g (1lb 2oz) leeks, thoroughly washed, trimmed and cut into 5cm (2in) batons
40g (1½oz) coarse sea salt

FOR THE SEASONING PASTE

10g (⅓oz) mustard seeds
30g (1oz) gochugaru
2 tbsp anchovy fish sauce, or 2 tbsp kelp water with ½ tsp salt
30g (1oz) garlic, grated
30g (1oz) ginger, grated
100g (3½oz) daikon, julienned

Serving Suggestions

- Perfect alongside braised meats or sausages.
- Pairs well with stews, dals or curries.
- Stir into broths or soups for instant depth and body.
- Spooned over warm rice with a fried egg for a simple winter meal

Kimmy's Notes

- **Spicing:** Toasting the mustard seeds is essential – it brings out nuttiness and tames bitterness.
- **Fermentation speed:** Leeks ferment quickly due to their soft texture; taste after just 24 hours.
- **Balance:** For a slightly sweeter variation, add 1–2 teaspoons of grated pear or apple to the paste.

This kimchi brings together the gentle sweetness of leeks with the warmth of mustard seeds, creating a ferment that feels almost Indian-spiced, yet is deeply Korean at heart. Leeks absorb seasoning beautifully, softening into silky batons that carry garlic, ginger and chilli flavours through every bite

Toasted mustard seeds add a surprising dimension: nutty, aromatic and lightly pungent, they transform the paste into something warmer and more complex. This kimchi ferments quickly, becoming tangy within a day or two, and develops further depth over the next week. It's a brilliant winter ferment, excellent with braised meats, lentil stews or even spooned into soups for extra flavour.

1. Salt leeks: Place the leeks in a bowl with the salt. Toss to coat, then leave for 30 minutes until softened. Drain in a colander but do not rinse.

2. Toast mustard seeds: In a small dry pan over a medium heat, toast the mustard seeds gently for 1–2 minutes until aromatic and popping. Remove from the heat and allow to cool.

3. Make paste: In the same large bowl as you salted the leeks, mix the gochugaru, fish sauce (or kelp water), garlic, ginger, toasted mustard seeds and daikon until it forms a thick paste.

4. Combine: Add the drained leeks to the paste and, wearing gloves, mix gently with your hands, coating each piece thoroughly.

5. Pack jar: Transfer to a clean jar, pressing down to remove air pockets. Leave 2cm (¾in) of headspace. Wipe the rim and seal.

6. Ferment: Leave at room temperature (18–22°C/ 65–70°F) for 1–3 days. When lightly tangy, tighten the lid and refrigerate. Flavour will deepen over the following week.

7. Store: Burp the jar daily for the first 7 days, and enjoy within 1–2 weeks.

Winter Root Vegetable Kimchi

Prep: 30 minutes
Brining: 1 hour
Fermentation: 3–5 days at room temperature before refrigeration
Makes: 2 litre (3½ pint) jar

300g (10½oz) swede, peeled and cut into 1cm (½in) cubes
300g (10½oz) celeriac, peeled and cut into matchsticks
300g (10½oz) Jerusalem artichokes, scrubbed and thinly sliced into rounds
300g (10½oz) turnips, scrubbed and cut into batons or wedges
40g (1½oz) coarse sea salt

FOR THE SEASONING PASTE

50g (1¾oz) gochugaru
2 tbsp anchovy fish sauce, or 2 tbsp kelp water with ½ tsp salt
30g (1oz) garlic, grated
15g (½oz) ginger, grated
20g (¾oz) spring onion, finely sliced

Kimmy's Notes

- **Fermentation speed:** In warmer kitchens, check from day 2; in cooler ones, fermentation might not get underway until day 5.
- **Variation:** Add thin batons of carrot or parsnip for additional sweetness.

A deep, crunchy, cold-weather ferment that transforms hearty roots into a rustic, sour and savoury pantry staple. Each vegetable softens at different rates and brings its own character: swede's nuttiness, celeriac's earthiness, Jerusalem artichoke's sweet crispness, and turnip's peppery bite. Together they create a kimchi with texture, depth and an unmistakably wintry feel.

1. Salt: Place swede, celeriac, Jerusalem artichokes and turnips in a large bowl. Sprinkle with salt, toss well and leave for 1 hour to draw out moisture. Drain thoroughly but do not rinse.

2. Make paste: In the same large bowl, mix the gochugaru, fish sauce (or kelp water), garlic, ginger and spring onion into a spreadable paste.

3. Mix: Return the drained vegetables to the bowl and add the seasoning paste. Wearing gloves, massage the veg to coat each piece evenly.

4. Pack jar: Transfer mixture to a clean jar, pressing down firmly to remove air pockets. Leave 2cm (¾in) of headspace. Wipe the rim and seal.

5. Ferment: Leave at room temperature for 3–5 days, depending on your kitchen's warmth. Taste daily; once tangy to your liking, move to the refrigerator.

6. Store: Burp the jar daily for the first 7 days. Keep chilled for 4–6 weeks. It will develop stronger sourness with time.

Serving Suggestions

- As a rustic side with rice porridge (juk).
- Alongside fatty winter stews or braised meats as a sour and crunchy lift.
- Chopped into grain bowls or folded into warm lentils for earthy contrast.

Using Fresh Kimchi (1–6 Days Old)

Fresh kimchi, between 1 and 5 days old, is the very beginning of the fermentation journey. At this stage, the vegetables remain crisp and juicy, more like a seasoned salad than a matured ferment. The flavours are clean and vivid: garlic and ginger are sharp, chilli heat is bright and the brine is lightly salty with only the faintest tang. By days 3 to 5, a gentle fizz may appear in the liquid – the first sign of lactic acid bacteria waking up and beginning their quiet transformation. In Korea, this stage is often called geotjeori, literally 'fresh kimchi'.

Eating kimchi young is a reminder that fermentation is alive from the very first day. It is best eaten raw, served as a banchan beside a steaming bowl of rice or grilled meats. It also works beautifully in simple salads and slaws, folded into cold noodle dishes or scattered over grain bowls for colour and crunch. A spoonful of fresh kimchi can even brighten sandwiches or wraps, while a quick toss in a hot pan turns it into a lively addition to stir-fries without losing its texture.

This is kimchi in its most youthful form: crisp, vibrant and fleeting. It captures the spirit of freshness, offering a taste of transformation in progress. To enjoy kimchi young is to celebrate its immediacy – food that is raw, spirited and alive, before its deeper layers of flavour emerge.

Kimchi Avocado Toast

VEGAN

Serves 2

2 slices of sourdough or wholegrain bread
1 tbsp olive oil
1 ripe avocado
80g (2¾oz) fresh napa kimchi, finely chopped, plus 1 tsp kimchi brine
Sea salt and black pepper
Pinch of chilli flakes or gochugaru, to serve
10g (⅓oz) microgreens or chopped chives, to serve

Kimchi avocado toast takes a modern brunch favourite and gives it a bold Korean twist. The creamy richness of ripe avocado meets the tangy, spicy crunch of young kimchi, all layered over golden, crisp sourdough. The contrast of textures – smooth avocado, crisp bread and juicy kimchi – makes every bite vibrant and balanced. A drizzle of kimchi brine adds depth, while microgreens or chives brighten the finish. It's quick to make, nourishing, satisfying and perfect for breakfast, a light lunch or a midday snack. You could even add a fried or poached egg or drizzle of sesame oil for a heartier version.

1. Toast bread: Brush both sides of each bread slice with the olive oil. Toast in a skillet for 2–3 minutes per side until golden and crisp.

2. Prepare avocado: Halve and pit the avocado. Scoop the flesh into a small bowl and mash lightly with a fork, leaving some chunks for texture. Season with salt, pepper and kimchi brine for extra tang, before giving it a final mix.

3. Assemble: Spread the seasoned avocado evenly over each slice of toasted bread. Divide the chopped kimchi between the slices, letting the juices mingle with the avocado.

4. Finish and serve: Sprinkle with chilli flakes or gochugaru, add a final crack of black pepper and garnish with microgreens or chopped chives.

Kimchi Summer Rolls with Chogochujang Sauce

VEGETARIAN

Makes 8 rolls

150g (5¼oz) fresh napa kimchi, or white kimchi, lightly drained and chopped
100g (3½oz) red cabbage, finely shredded
80g (2¾oz) carrot, julienned
80g (2¾oz) cucumber, julienned
1 avocado, sliced (optional)
10g (⅓oz) fresh coriander leaves
10g (⅓oz) fresh mint leaves
100g (3½oz) cooked vermicelli noodles (optional)
8 rice paper wrappers, about 22cm (8½in) diameter

FOR THE CHOGOCHUJANG SAUCE

50g (1¾oz) gochujang
2 tbsp rice vinegar (or apple cider vinegar)
2 tsp honey
1 garlic clove, grated (optional)
1 tsp toasted sesame oil

Fresh, cool and bursting with tangy crunch, these kimchi summer rolls are a light and refreshing way to enjoy kimchi in warm weather. Crisp vegetables, fragrant herbs, soft noodles and young kimchi are wrapped inside delicate rice papers, creating a vibrant roll that's as nourishing as it is satisfying. Served with a simple seasoned gochujang dipping sauce, they're perfect as a snack, appetiser or a colourful addition to a shared meal.

---

1. Prepare filling: Arrange the kimchi, vegetables, herbs and vermicelli, if using, into separate piles for easy assembly.

2. Soften wrappers: Fill a shallow dish with warm water. Dip one rice paper wrapper into the water for 4–5 seconds, until just pliable but not too soft. Lay flat on a clean damp tea towel or board.

3. Layer and roll: Place a few coriander and mint leaves in the centre of the wrapper. Add a spoonful of kimchi, then layer carrot, cucumber, red cabbage, avocado slices and vermicelli, if using. Fold the bottom of the wrapper over the filling, tuck in the sides, and roll tightly away from you until sealed. Repeat with the remaining wrappers until they're all filled.

4. Make dipping sauce: Mix the gochujang, vinegar and honey together until smooth, then stir in the garlic and sesame oil. Taste and adjust the balance to your preference.

5. Serve: Arrange the summer rolls neatly on a platter. Serve immediately with the dipping sauce for dipping or drizzling.

Kimchi Tofu Scramble on Toast

VEGAN

Serves 2

200g (7oz) firm tofu
1 tbsp rapeseed or sesame oil
80g (2¾oz) fresh napa kimchi, finely chopped, plus 1–2 tsp kimchi brine, if needed
1 spring onion, finely sliced, white and green parts kept separate
½ tsp ground turmeric
1 tbsp light soy sauce or tamari
Pinch of black pepper
2 slices of sourdough or rye bread, toasted
1 avocado, sliced (optional)
Pinch of toasted sesame seeds, to garnish (optional)
Pinch of gochugaru flakes, to garnish (optional)

This is a quick, plant-based twist on scrambled eggs that manages to feel both hearty and refreshing. Firm tofu gives body and substance, while mid-fermented kimchi cuts through with brightness, spice and crunch. The combination transforms a simple scramble into something bold, colourful and deeply satisfying.

Turmeric adds golden colour and warmth, while soy sauce enhances the savoury base. Served on toasted sourdough or rye, this dish makes a filling breakfast, brunch or even a light supper. It's endlessly adaptable – add spinach, peppers or mushrooms, or, as I've suggested here, scatter some sesame seeds or a pinch of gochugaru to finish. Quick to prepare, comforting yet nutritious, it's the kind of everyday recipe that never feels ordinary.

1. Prepare tofu: Drain and pat dry the tofu using kitchen paper or a clean tea towel. Crumble into uneven chunks resembling scrambled eggs.

2. Cook aromatics: Heat oil in a pan over medium heat. When it's hot, fry the kimchi and spring onion whites for 1–2 minutes until fragrant.

3. Season and colour: Stir in the turmeric, then add the tofu. Cook for 3–4 minutes, stirring regularly while letting the edges of the tofu brown lightly.

4. Flavour: Add soy sauce and a pinch of black pepper. Stir well and taste, adjusting seasoning with more soy sauce or a spoonful of kimchi brine if needed.

5. Serve: Pile the scramble onto hot toast. Garnish with the spring onion greens and sesame seeds and/or gochugaru, if using. Serve with the avocado slices on the toast or on the side.

Stir-fried Kimchi Udon with Greens

VEGAN

Serves 2–3

400g (14oz) udon noodles (fresh or frozen; if dried, adjust cooking time)
2 tbsp rapeseed oil, plus extra for drizzling
1 small onion, thinly sliced
2 garlic cloves, finely sliced
200g (7oz) young kimchi (3–6 days old works best), chopped, plus 3 tbsp kimchi brine (optional)
30g (1oz) gochujang
1 tbsp soy sauce or tamari
1 tsp sugar (optional)
5g (⅛in) gochugaru (optional, for extra heat)
150g (5¼oz) leafy greens (spinach, pak choi or kale), roughly chopped
30g (1oz) spring onions, sliced diagonally
2 tsp toasted sesame oil
Sea salt and black pepper
10g (⅓oz) toasted sesame seeds, to garnish

This is a quick, comforting dish that brings together the chewy bite of udon noodles with the bright crunch of fresh kimchi and the tenderness of seasonal greens. Instead of relying on the tang of aged kimchi, this version is lighter, fresher and more vegetable-forward, making it perfect for summer evenings or when you want something warming without heaviness. Fresh kimchi stir-fries differently: it softens just enough in the pan to release its aromatics, but still keeps some crispness. If you want to try the deeper, tangier flavour of tradition, try the same recipe with aged kimchi (3+ weeks old). Both versions shine in their own way.

1. Prepare the noodles: Bring a pot of salted water to the boil over a high heat. Reduce the heat to medium and cook the udon until just tender according to the packet instructions. For fresh or frozen, this should be 2–3 minutes. For dried, slightly undercook them so they don't become mushy when stir-frying. Drain and rinse briefly under cold water to stop the cooking, then toss with a drizzle of oil to prevent sticking.

2. Make the base: Heat the rapeseed oil in a frying pan or wok over a medium heat. Add the onion and cook for 3–4 minutes until softened. Stir in the garlic and cook for 30 seconds until fragrant.

3. Add the kimchi: Stir in the chopped kimchi and fry for 2–3 minutes until sizzling and slightly caramelised. Add the kimchi brine if using, letting it bubble and coat the vegetables.

4. Add seasoning: Stir in gochujang, soy sauce and sugar, if it's needed to balance the kimchi. Add the gochugaru if you want some extra heat. Mix until everything is well coated.

5. Cook the greens: Add the leafy greens and cook just until wilted but still vibrant. Toss in most of the spring onions, saving a few for garnish.

6. Combine with noodles: Add the drained noodles to the pan. Toss everything together, adding a splash of noodle water if the pan feels dry. Drizzle with sesame oil, then season with salt and pepper, to taste.

7. Finish and serve: Divide into bowls, garnish with toasted sesame seeds and the reserved spring onions.

Using Mid-fermented Kimchi (1–3 Weeks Old)

In 1 to 3 weeks, kimchi enters its mid-fermentation stage – the point at which it becomes the most versatile. The flavours are no longer raw and sharp but rounded and balanced: the garlic and ginger have softened, the chilli heat has mellowed and a bold tang begins to dominate. The brine grows fizzy and complex, a sign of thriving lactic acid bacteria, while the texture shifts from firm and crunchy to tender with a bit of bite. This is kimchi in motion, alive and energetic, full of savoury depth without tipping into the pungency of older jars.

Mid-ferment kimchi is beloved because it suits almost everything. It can still be eaten raw as a banchan, where its tang cuts beautifully through a warm bowl of rice or grilled meat. But it also excels in cooking, where its sourness and umami lift simple dishes to another level. A couple of spoonfuls of kimchi tossed into fried rice brings brightness and spice. A ladleful stirred into jjigae (kimchi stew) gives body and depth. Chopped mid-ferment kimchi works as a filling for dumplings or pancakes, folded into noodle dishes or even layered with cheese in a toasted sandwich for a sharp, savoury kick.

This stage is where kimchi comes into its own – bold enough to transform dishes but still vibrant enough to enjoy fresh.

Kimchi & Quinoa One-pot Stew

VEGAN

Serves 4

1 tbsp vegetable oil
1 small onion, finely chopped
20g (¾oz) garlic, grated
15g (½oz) ginger, grated
200g (7oz) mid-fermented kimchi, roughly chopped, plus 2 tbsp kimchi brine
1 pepper, diced
1 tsp gochugaru (optional)
170g (6oz) quinoa, rinsed well
1 litre (1¾ pints) vegetable stock
100g (3½oz) baby spinach or kale, roughly chopped
1 tsp toasted sesame oil
Black pepper
2 spring onions, thinly sliced, to garnish
Toasted sesame seeds, to garnish (optional)

This modern one-pot brings Korean comfort and a global grain together. Quinoa isn't traditional in Korea, but its light nuttiness pairs beautifully with the tang of mid-fermented kimchi. Simmered with vegetables and stock, the grains soak up kimchi's sour depth, creating a hearty yet balanced stew. The live cultures don't survive cooking, but the flavours of fermentation remain, giving a broth that's warming, restorative and easy enough to make for a weeknight supper. It is also endlessly customisable; try adding mushrooms, courgettes or butternut squash for a different flavour, or add shredded chicken, tofu or a poached egg for extra protein.

1. Sauté aromatics: Heat the oil in a large heavy-based pot over a medium heat. Add the onion, garlic and ginger. Cook for 3–4 minutes, stirring occasionally, until softened and fragrant.

2. Make base: Stir in the chopped kimchi, kimchi brine and pepper. Cook for 3–4 minutes, allowing the vegetables to soften and the kimchi to release its tangy aroma. Add gochugaru if you'd like more spice.

3. Add quinoa and stock: Stir the quinoa into the pot, coating it well in the kimchi mixture. Pour in the stock. Bring to a gentle boil, then reduce the heat to low.

4. Simmer stew: Cover and simmer for 15–18 minutes, stirring once or twice, until the quinoa is tender and most of the liquid has been absorbed. Add a splash of hot water if you prefer a soupier consistency.

5. Finish with greens: Stir in the spinach or kale along with the toasted sesame oil. Cook for another 1–2 minutes until the greens have just wilted. Season lightly with black pepper, to taste.

6. Serve: Ladle into bowls and garnish with sliced spring onions and sesame seeds, if you like.

Kimchi Grilled Cheese Sandwich

VEGETARIAN OPTION

Serves 2

4 slices of sourdough bread, less than 1cm (½in) thick
20g (¾oz) unsalted butter, softened
120g (4¼oz) mid-fermented napa kimchi, lightly drained and finely chopped
Pinch of gochugaru or chilli flakes (optional)
80g (2¾oz) Red Leicester or mature Cheddar, grated
70g (2½oz) mozzarella, thinly sliced
2 tsp neutral oil (optional)
1 spring onion, finely sliced, to garnish (optional)

Kimchi grilled cheese is comfort food with a bold twist: molten, gooey cheese encasing the tangy, spicy crunch of kimchi, all held together by crisp golden bread. At first bite, you get the indulgence of a classic toastie, but then the kimchi cuts through with its sour, fiery and complex flavours, bringing balance to the richness. This dish shines when made with kimchi that has fermented for 2–4 weeks, when its flavour is bright yet deeply sour. Using both sliced mozzarella for stretch and a good red cheese – like Red Leicester – or mature Cheddar for sharpness creates the perfect balance of creamy melt and savoury bite. It pairs brilliantly with tomato soup, pickles or a cold beer.

1. Prepare bread: Lay the sourdough slices on a board. Spread butter evenly over one side of each slice – this will be the side facing the pan for crispness.

2. Assemble filling: In a small bowl, mix the chopped kimchi with gochugaru, if you want extra spice. Keep the cheese ready in two piles.

3. Layer sandwich: Place two slices of bread butter side down. Divide most of the grated Red Leicester or Cheddar between the slices, then top with the kimchi, followed by the mozzarella slices. Finish by dividing the rest of the grated cheese between the two, then top with the remaining bread slices, butter side out.

4. Cook: Heat a skillet over medium-low, and add the oil, if you like, for extra crispness. Place the sandwiches in the pan. Cook for 3–4 minutes per side, pressing gently with a spatula, until the bread is golden brown and the cheese has fully melted. Adjust heat down to avoid over-browning before the cheese melts through, if necessary.

5. Serve: Transfer the sandwiches to a cutting board, rest for 1 minute to let the cheese settle slightly, then slice diagonally, garnish with spring onions, and serve hot.

Budae Jjigae (Army Stew)
부대찌개

Serves 4–5

200g (7oz) Spam or canned ham, sliced
200g (7oz) Korean sausages (or frankfurters), diagonally sliced
150g (5¼oz) pork belly, cut into thin strips
200g (7oz) mid-fermented kimchi (2–3 weeks old), roughly chopped
100–120g (3½–4¼oz) baked beans (optional)
150g (5¼oz) firm tofu, sliced into slabs
60g (2oz) carrot, thinly sliced into half-moons
60g (2oz) spring onions, cut into 5cm (2in) batons
60g (2oz) mushrooms (enoki, oyster or button), trimmed
1 x pack of instant ramen noodles (or udon/somyeon as substitutes)
1 slice of American cheese (optional)

FOR THE BROTH

2 tbsp gochugaru
1 tbsp gochujang
1 tbsp Korean soy sauce for soup (guk-ganjang) or Japanese usukuchi soy sauce, or light soy sauce
1 tbsp rice wine or mirin
15g (½oz) garlic, grated
2.5cm (1in) ginger, grated
1.5 litres (2½ pints) water or light anchovy or beef stock
Sea salt and black pepper

Army Stew, or budae jjigae, was born in the years after the Korean War, when resourceful cooks combined local spice and kimchi with surplus rations from U.S. military bases. Spam, canned sausages and sometimes baked beans – foreign to the Korean palate – found their way into bubbling pots alongside gochugaru, gochujang and well-fermented kimchi. What began as makeshift sustenance soon became a dish of resilience and ingenuity.

Today, budae jjigae is a beloved comfort food, cooked in homes and pubs across Korea. It is fiery and hearty, improvised yet deeply communal, with each pot carrying memory as well as flavour. Its balance lies in contrast: heavy meats cut through by kimchi's acidity, fiery broth mellowed by noodles and even a melting slice of cheese. Around the pot, friends and family scoop steaming bowls that nourish body, spirit and togetherness.

1. Make seasoning base: In a small bowl, mix together gochugaru, gochujang, soy sauce, rice wine, garlic, ginger and a pinch of black pepper into a thick paste.

2. Assemble pot: In a wide stew pot, arrange the meats, kimchi, baked beans, tofu and vegetables in sections around the pot. Place the seasoning paste in the centre. Pour in broth until the ingredients are mostly submerged. (Set ramen aside for later.)

3. Cook the stew: Bring the pot to a boil over medium-high heat. As the broth heats, the seasoning paste will dissolve, turning the stew a deep scarlet. Simmer for 10–15 minutes until the pork belly is cooked through and flavours have melded.

4. Add noodles: In the last 3–4 minutes, add the ramen noodles directly into the pot. Cook until just chewy.

5. Finish and serve: Taste the broth and adjust the seasoning with salt and pepper if needed. Lay the slice of cheese on the top, if you like. Transfer the pot to the centre of the table, preferably over a tabletop burner to keep it simmering. Ladle into bowls and serve with steamed rice on the side.

Kimchi & Potato Gratin

VEGETARIAN OPTION

Serves 4

200ml (7fl oz) single cream
1 garlic clove, grated
1 tsp vegetable oil, for greasing
500g (1lb 2oz) waxy potatoes (e.g. Charlotte), peeled and thinly sliced
100g (3½oz) mid-fermented napa kimchi, chopped
50g (1¾oz) mature Cheddar or Gruyère, grated
1 tsp gochugaru (optional)
Sea salt and black pepper

Kimchi and potato gratin takes the familiar comfort of a creamy potato bake and transforms it with the bold vibrancy of kimchi. Thin slices of potato are layered with kimchi, cream, garlic and cheese, then baked until bubbling and golden. The result is rich and indulgent, yet lifted by kimchi's tang and spice.

Mid-fermented kimchi is ideal as it brightens the dish without overpowering the cream. Waxy potatoes such as Charlotte or Yukon Gold hold their shape, soaking up flavour while staying tender. Cheese adds the savoury backbone: Cheddar for sharpness or Gruyère for nutty depth. This gratin is versatile enough to serve as a main with salad or as a side to roasts, and it reheats beautifully, making it practical as well as delicious

1. Preheat oven: Preheat the oven to 180°C/160°C Fan/350°F/Gas 4.

2. Prepare cream mixture: In a bowl, combine the cream with the garlic, a pinch of salt and a grind of black pepper. Mix well so the garlic can infuse.

3. Assemble first layer: Lightly grease the baking dish with the oil. Arrange half of the potato slices in overlapping layers along the bottom of the dish.

4. Add kimchi and cream: Spread the chopped kimchi evenly over the potatoes. Spoon several tablespoons of the cream mixture over the top.

5. Add second potato layer: Arrange the remaining potatoes neatly on top, again overlapping slightly. Pour over the rest of the cream mixture, ensuring the potatoes are coated.

6. Add cheese and spice: Scatter the grated Cheddar or Gruyère over the top, then sprinkle with the gochugaru, if you like, for an extra fiery kick.

7. Bake covered: Cover the dish with foil and place in the preheated oven. Bake for 25 minutes, until the potatoes have softened.

8. Bake uncovered: Remove the foil and bake for a further 20 minutes, until the surface is golden and bubbling, and the potatoes are tender when pierced with a knife.

9. Rest and serve: Let the gratin rest for 5 minutes before serving so the layers settle.

Kimchi Mac & Cheese

VEGETARIAN OPTION

Serves 4 as a main, 6 as a side

300g (10½oz) macaroni (or another short pasta such as rigatoni or penne)
1 tsp olive oil, for drizzling
30g (1oz) unsalted butter
30g (1oz) plain flour
500ml (17½fl oz) whole milk, warmed
150g (5¼oz) mature Cheddar, grated
40g (1½oz) Red Leicester, grated, plus extra for topping
50g (1¾oz) mozzarella, torn or grated
1 tsp gochugaru (optional)
150g (5¼oz) mid-fermented napa kimchi, chopped and lightly squeezed, plus 1 tbsp kimchi brine (optional)
Sea salt and black pepper

FOR THE TOPPING (OPTIONAL)

40g panko breadcrumbs
30g olive oil or melted butter
40g Red Leicester, grated

Kimchi mac and cheese is a dish where two comfort-food worlds collide: the creamy, molten luxury of classic macaroni and cheese and the tangy crunch and subtle spice of kimchi. Mid-fermented kimchi works best here. At this stage it has the right balance of acidity and texture – sour enough to cut through cheese, but not so sharp that it overpowers the sauce. Each bite is layered: the soft pasta coated in rich, velvety cheese; the kimchi adding surprise crunch and a spark of heat; the optional topping giving a golden crust.

---

1. Preheat the oven: If baking to finish, preheat the oven to 200°C/180°C Fan/400°F/Gas 6.

2. Cook pasta: Bring a large saucepan of salted water to the boil over a high heat. Add the macaroni and cook until just al dente – slightly firm in the middle. Drain in a colander, toss with a drizzle of oil to prevent it sticking together, then set aside.

3. Make cheese sauce: In a saucepan, melt the butter over a medium heat. Add the flour and stir constantly for about 1 minute to form a roux. Gradually add the warmed milk, whisking continuously to avoid lumps. Simmer gently until the sauce thickens, around 5–7 minutes. Remove from the heat and stir in the three cheeses. Stir until the cheese has melted and the sauce is smooth and glossy. Season with salt and pepper, and the gochugaru if you want an extra kick.

4. Incorporate kimchi: Gently fold in the kimchi, ensuring it's evenly distributed. Then stir in the drained pasta, mixing well. Taste, and if you want a deeper tang, you can stir in a spoonful of kimchi brine.

5. Bake for a golden finish (optional): Transfer the pasta and sauce mixture into a baking dish. In a small bowl, mix the breadcrumbs with the olive oil or melted butter until lightly coated. Sprinkle over the pasta along with the remaining Red Leicester. Bake for 20 minutes until golden, crunchy and bubbling around the edges.

6. Serve: Allow to rest for 2–3 minutes before serving – it will thicken slightly as it cools.

7. Store: Any leftovers will keep in the fridge for up to 3 days. Reheat gently in the oven or on the hob with a splash of milk stirred through to restore creaminess.

Kimchi & Cheese Empanadas

VEGETARIAN

Makes 12

FOR THE DOUGH

300g (10½oz) plain flour
1 tsp salt
100g (3½oz) cold unsalted butter or lard, diced
1 egg
1 tsp white wine vinegar, apple cider vinegar or lemon juice
80–100ml (3–3½fl oz) cold water

Empanadas are one of the world's great comfort foods – portable, hand-sized pies with flaky pastry and savoury fillings. From Argentina to Spain, from street markets to home kitchens, each culture adapts them to local tastes. In this version, kimchi brings the unexpected spark. Its tangy, spicy crunch cuts through the richness of molten cheese.

They travel well for picnics, taste delicious cold in a lunchbox and can be frozen ahead for quick meals. Unlike some pastries that lose their appeal once cooled, the punchy kimchi flavour keeps these empanadas lively hours after baking.

There are two parts to this recipe – making the empanada casing dough and then making the empanadas themselves. You can also source empanada discs from select stores should you wish to skip making the dough yourself.

---

1. Mix dry ingredients: In a large bowl, whisk together flour and salt.

2. Add fat: Rub in the cold butter or lard with your fingertips until the mixture looks like coarse crumbs.

3. Bind with liquid: Add the egg, vinegar or lemon juice and most of the water. Mix gently with a fork until the dough begins to come together. Add more water if needed – it should hold together but not be sticky.

4. Knead briefly: Turn onto a lightly floured surface and knead for 1–2 minutes until smooth. Don't overwork or the pastry will become tough.

5. Rest: Wrap in cling film and chill the dough for at least 30 minutes before using. This relaxes the gluten and firms up the butter or lard to improve flakiness.

6. Store: You can keep the dough, well wrapped in cling film, in the fridge for 3 days, or in the freezer, wrapped in cling film and sealed in a freezer bag, for up to 2 months. Just defrost thoroughly in the fridge before using.

FOR THE EMPANADAS

1 tbsp rapeseed or sunflower oil
1 small onion, finely diced
250g (8¾oz) mid-fermented kimchi, well drained and finely chopped
200g (7oz) mozzarella, grated (or half mozzarella, half mature Cheddar for a stronger flavour)
50g (1¾oz) cream cheese (optional)
½ tsp sea salt, or to taste
¼ tsp black pepper
½ tsp smoked paprika or gochugaru (optional)
Small handful fresh coriander or chives, finely chopped (optional)
1 egg, beaten, to glaze (optional)
Vegetable oil, for deep frying

1. Preheat oven (optional): If baking instead of deep frying, preheat the oven to 200°C/180°C Fan/400°F/Gas 6.

2. Prepare filling: Heat the oil in a frying pan over a medium heat. Add the diced onion and sauté for about 5 minutes until translucent. Stir in the chopped kimchi and cook for 2–3 minutes to reduce excess liquid. Remove from the heat and allow to cool.

3. Combine with cheese: In a large bowl, mix the cooled kimchi-onion mixture with the grated mozzarella and cream cheese, if using. Taste for saltiness, then add salt, if needed, followed by pepper, paprika or gochugaru and herbs, if using. Stir until the mixture is cohesive.

4. Shape empanadas: If using shop-bought empanada discs, lay them out on your work surface. If using homemade dough, tip out onto a lightly floured work surface and roll out the dough to 3mm (⅛in) thickness. Cut into 10–12cm (4–5in) circles using a cookie cutter or by cutting around a small plate. Place a heaped tablespoonful of filling in the centre of each circle. Fold the pastry over to form a half-moon shape. Press the edges firmly to seal (dab with a little water, if needed), then crimp with a fork or pleat by hand for a traditional look.

5. Cook empanadas: To bake them, arrange them on a lined baking tray. Brush the tops with the beaten egg and bake for 20–25 minutes until golden brown. Alternatively, to deep fry them, heat 5–7cm (2–3in) of oil in a deep, heavy-bottomed pan to 170°C (340°F). Fry the empanadas in small batches, 3–4 minutes per side, until crisp and golden. Remove from the oil using a slotted spoon and drain on kitchen paper. Repeat with the remaining empanadas.

6. Cool and serve: Rest the empanadas for 5–10 minutes before serving. This helps the filling set slightly, so the cheese doesn't spill out on the first bite.

7. Store: Freeze unbaked empanadas. Place on a tray in the freezer until solid, then bag. Bake from frozen at 200°C/180°C Fan/400°F/Gas 6, adding about 5 minutes to the cooking time.

Using Well-fermented Kimchi (3–6 Weeks or More)

After 3 weeks, kimchi enters its well-fermented stage, where flavours become strong, layered and deeply savoury. The once-crisp leaves are now tender and pliable, infused with a sharp, almost wine-like acidity. Garlic and ginger fade into the background while umami rises, creating a flavour profile that is bold and complex. The brine is concentrated and aromatic, carrying the tang of lactic acid along with deep, almost cheesy undertones.

At this stage, Koreans often call it shin-kimchi (sour, well-fermented kimchi). True mukeunji, the deeply aged kimchi beloved for braises and stews, refers to jars kept for many months, sometimes even a year or more. Both, however, represent a shift from freshness towards depth, treasured not for crunch but for the layers of flavour they bring to the table.

Well-fermented kimchi is less about eating raw and more about cooking. Its powerful sourness and softened texture make it a transformative ingredient, capable of anchoring entire dishes. A pot of kimchi jjigae made with mature kimchi has a richness that fresh jars simply cannot match. Braised pork wrapped with old kimchi becomes tender and aromatic. Pancakes filled with deeply fermented cabbage develop complexity with every bite. Even a spoonful blended into sauces, broths or pasta dishes can bring unexpected depth.

This is kimchi for winter evenings and hearty meals that need grounding and warmth. What it lacks in brightness, it offers in resilience: pungent, soulful and endlessly nourishing. To cook with it is to understand the full power of fermentation – not just preservation but transformation. A jar that no longer whispers of beginnings, but carries the memory of weeks past, offering depth that turns even the simplest dish into something special.

Vegan Kimchi Mandu Jeongol
김치만두전골

VEGAN

Serves 5–6

FOR THE BROTH

1.5 litres (2½ pints) vegetable stock (or kelp-mushroom broth)
4 tbsp kimchi brine
1½ tbsp soy sauce
30–50g (1–1¾oz) gochugaru, to taste
30g (1oz) garlic, grated
Sea salt

FOR THE HOTPOT

375g (13oz) well-fermented kimchi, chopped
300g (10½oz) napa cabbage, cut into bite-size pieces
1 courgette, sliced into half-moons
5–6 shiitake mushrooms, thinly sliced
300g (10½oz) firm tofu, cubed
1 quantity of Vegan Kimchi Mandu (page 178)
4 spring onions, sliced

DIPPING SAUCE
(PER PERSON, OPTIONAL)

2 tbsp soy sauce
1 tbsp rice vinegar
Pinch of gochugaru

This spicy kimchi dumpling hotpot is the kind of dish that turns a table into a celebration. Dumplings, kimchi, vegetables and tofu simmer together in one steaming pot placed at the centre for everyone to share. Jeongol is more than just soup – it is a communal ritual, meant to be lingered over, with broth ladled out and topped up as the meal unfolds.

For many families in Korea, it is tied to winter memories: steam on the windows, dumplings bobbing in the broth, children fishing them out first. Today it is as joyful as ever, and I often make it with my vegan mandu (page 178) – a pot of warmth, memory and kimchi in every spoonful. Serve with steamed rice and light banchan such as cucumber kimchi (page 97), seasoned spinach or pickled radish, or add glass noodles (dangmyeon) or sliced rice cakes (tteok) in the last 5 minutes for a heartier hotpot.

---

1. Prepare broth: In a wide shallow pot, bring the vegetable stock to a simmer. Stir in the kimchi brine, soy sauce, gochugaru, to taste, garlic and a pinch of salt.

2. Layer vegetables and tofu: Add the chopped kimchi, napa cabbage, courgette, mushrooms and tofu. Simmer for 7–8 minutes, until the vegetables soften slightly

3. Add dumplings: Gently place the dumplings on top of the vegetables. Cover with a lid and simmer for 5–6 minutes if the mandu have just been made, or 10–12 minutes if cooking from chilled. Check they are hot through.

4. Make dipping sauce (optional): Mix together the dipping sauce ingredients and divide into individual small serving bowls.

5. Finish and serve: Scatter with the spring onions. Serve the whole pot at the table with a ladle, accompanied by the dipping sauce, if using.

Kimmy's Notes

- Squeeze fillings thoroughly (kimchi, tofu, sprouts) to avoid soggy dumplings.
- Dumplings freeze well uncooked: freeze on a tray, then bag.

Kimchi-mari Guksu (Noodles in Cold Kimchi Brine) 김치말이국수

VEGAN

Serves 2

200g (7oz) somyeon (소면) noodles
300ml (10½fl oz) well-fermented kimchi brine (napa kimchi or dongchimi)

TO ADJUST SEASONING (OPTIONAL)

Ice cubes (made from cooled, boiled water, to avoid cloudiness)
½ tsp sugar
½ tsp Korean mustard (gyeoja) or rice vinegar
Pinch of salt

TO GARNISH (OPTIONAL)

100g (3½oz) kimchi, chopped
½ cucumber, julienned
½ pear, thinly sliced
1 boiled egg, halved

In Korea, cold noodles have long been a way to endure the heat of summer and savour the gifts of fermentation. Naengmyeon (냉면), with its buckwheat noodles and icy beef or dongchimi broth, is the most famous example. Once a winter delicacy in the north, it has become a national dish enjoyed year-round. Guksu (국수), by contrast, belongs to the home. Everyday wheat noodles that can be tossed, souped or chilled, they reflect whatever the kitchen offers. Kimchi-mari guksu sits firmly in this tradition. Where naengmyeon carries ceremony and often appears in restaurants, kimchi-mari guksu feels improvised and intimate, a clever way to give new life to kimchi brine always waiting in the jar. Together they show two sides of Korea's noodle culture: one formal and celebrated, the other casual and resourceful, both designed to cool the body and refresh the spirit.

Kimchi-mari guksu is summer comfort food at its best: thin wheat noodles in icy kimchi brine. What many see as 'leftover juice' becomes a probiotic broth that is sharp, tangy and deeply refreshing. With dongchimi brine it is delicate and clear, almost like a fermented consommé; with red kimchi brine it is bold and spicy, garnished with cucumber, pear, kimchi and egg.

---

1. Cook noodles: Bring a large pan of water to the boil. Add somyeon and cook for 2–3 minutes, or according to packet instructions, until just tender. Drain and rinse thoroughly under cold running water, rubbing gently to remove surface starch. Drain well and set aside.

2. Prepare broth: Pour kimchi brine into a jug. Taste carefully and adjust to your preference. If it is too salty, dilute with cold water or ice; too sour, stir in a little sugar; or too flat: add a touch of mustard or vinegar and a pinch of salt.

3. Chill: Place in the fridge for at least 30 minutes to thoroughly chill, or serve immediately with ice cubes.

4. Assemble bowls: Divide the chilled noodles between two bowls. Ladle over the seasoned kimchi brine until just covering the noodles. Add a few ice cubes to each bowl, if you like.

5. Garnish and serve: Top with the garnishes of your choice: kimchi, cucumber, pear slices and/or half a boiled egg. Serve at once, before the ice fully melts.

Kimchi Bindaetteok
김치 빈대떡

VEGAN

300g (10½oz) dried mung beans (hulled if possible), soaked overnight in plenty of water
200ml (7fl oz) water
150g (5¼oz) well-fermented kimchi, chopped, plus 2-3 tbsp kimchi brine
½ onion, finely sliced
2 spring onions, finely chopped
1 garlic clove, grated
1 green chilli, deseeded and finely sliced (optional)
1 tsp coarse sea salt
Vegetable oil, for frying

FOR THE DIPPING SAUCE

2 tbsp soy sauce
1 tbsp rice vinegar
½ tsp gochugaru
½ tsp toasted sesame seeds

Mung bean pancakes are a long-standing Korean street and market food: nutty, savoury and hearty. In this version, well-fermented kimchi is mixed straight into the mung bean batter, adding tang, spice and depth. The result is a pancake that's crisp outside, creamy inside and rich with character. I love to eat them hot from the pan with a soy-based dipping sauce, and they are especially good with a glass of makgeolli.

1. Prepare batter: Drain the soaked mung beans. Transfer to a blender, add the fresh water and blend until mostly smooth but slightly textured. The batter should be thick enough to coat a spoon. Transfer to a mixing bowl

2. Build mixture: To the bowl with the batter, add in the chopped kimchi and its brine, the onion, spring onions, garlic and chilli, if you like. Add the salt and give everything a good stir.

3. Make dipping sauce: In a small bowl, combine the ingredients for the dipping sauce and set aside.

4. Fry pancakes: Heat 2-3 tablespoons of oil in a large skillet over medium-high heat. Ladle about 100ml (3½fl oz) of batter per pancake into the pan and spread into 10cm (4in) rounds. Cook for 3-4 minutes until the bottom is golden and edges are crisp. Flip carefully and cook the other side for 3-4 minutes until set in the centre. Place the cooked pancakes on a baking tray lined with parchment and keep them in a low oven (100°C/80°C Fan/200°F/Gas ¼). Cover loosely with foil to stop them drying out. Continue with the rest of the batter, adding a little oil between batches if needed.

5. Serve: Arrange the pancakes on a warm plate or cast-iron pan to keep them warm at the table, and serve with the dipping sauce.

Kimchi Baked Beans on Sourdough

VEGAN

Serves 2

1 tbsp olive oil
1 small onion, finely chopped
1 garlic clove, grated
100g (3½oz) well-fermented kimchi (3-6+ weeks), finely chopped, plus extra to serve, plus 2 tbsp kimchi brine (optional)
200g (7oz) passata or chopped tomatoes
1 tbsp tomato paste
1 tbsp light brown sugar or maple syrup
1 tsp smoked paprika
½ tsp chilli flakes, or to taste
1 x 400g (14oz) tin of haricot or navy beans, drained and rinsed, or 250g (8¾oz) dried beans, soaked overnight and cooked until tender
4 slices of sourdough bread
Olive oil or melted butter, for brushing
Sea salt and black pepper
Chives or spring onions, finely chopped, to garnish
Fresh or pickled chillies, to garnish (optional)

This dish is a bold twist on the familiar baked beans on toast, elevated with the depth and tang of aged kimchi. The sourness of well-fermented kimchi (3-6 weeks or older) balances beautifully with the sweetness of tomato and a hint of smoke from paprika. The beans soak up all the flavours, creating a hearty, saucy base that feels both comforting and new. Served on toasted sourdough, it becomes a meal that sits somewhere between brunch and comfort-food supper – a dish that warms you from the inside out while showcasing how kimchi can transform everyday staples.

1. Prepare base: Heat the olive oil in a medium saucepan over medium heat. Add the onion and cook, stirring regularly, for about 5 minutes until softened and translucent. Stir in the garlic and sauté briefly for 30 seconds until fragrant.

2. Make sauce: Add the chopped kimchi and fry for 2-3 minutes, letting it soften and release its tangy aroma. Stir in the passata, tomato paste, sugar or syrup, smoked paprika and chilli flakes. Add the kimchi brine if using, then season lightly with salt and pepper to taste.

3. Add beans: Fold in the drained beans gently, ensuring they are evenly coated in the sauce. Lower the heat and let simmer for 15-20 minutes, stirring occasionally, until the sauce thickens and the flavours have melded. Taste and adjust the seasoning – more sugar for balance, brine for tang or chilli flakes for heat.

4. Toast sourdough: While the beans simmer, toast the sourdough slices until crisp and golden. Brush lightly with olive oil or melted butter.

5. Assemble and serve: Put two slices of sourdough on each plate, and generously spoon over the hot kimchi baked beans. Top with extra chopped kimchi, a sprinkle of chives or spring onions, and fresh or pickled chillies, if you like. Serve immediately while the toast is crisp and the beans are bubbling hot.

Kimchi & Butter Pasta with Parmesan Crumbs

VEGETARIAN OPTION

Serves 2

200g (7oz) dried spaghetti or linguine
1 tbsp olive oil, plus extra for drizzling, if desired
50g (1¾oz) unsalted butter
1 garlic clove, thinly sliced
100g (3½oz) well-fermented kimchi (3–6+ weeks), finely chopped, plus 2 tbsp kimchi brine (optional)
Sea salt and black pepper

FOR THE PARMESAN CRUMBS

15g (½oz) unsalted butter
1 tbsp plain breadcrumbs
Pinch of gochugaru (optional)
50g (1¾oz) Parmesan, or vegetarian hard cheese, finely grated

TO GARNISH (OPTIONAL)

Kimchi or kimchi brine
Chives or spring onion greens, finely chopped

A quick, indulgent pasta that proves aged kimchi isn't only for stews and rice. Here, the rich nuttiness of butter and Parmesan meets the sharp tang of well-fermented kimchi, creating a sauce that clings beautifully to long noodles. The golden Parmesan crumbs add crunch and a salty kick, elevating this into a weeknight dish that feels restaurant-worthy.

1. Cook the pasta: Bring a large pot of salted water to a boil over a high heat. Add the spaghetti, reduce the heat to medium and cook until just al dente. Reserve 100ml (3½fl oz) of the cooking water, then drain. Toss the pasta with a drizzle of oil to prevent it sticking together, then set aside.

2. Make Parmesan crumbs: In a small frying pan over a medium heat, melt the butter. Add the breadcrumbs and chilli flakes, if using. Stir for 2–3 minutes until golden and crisp. Remove from the heat, then stir in the Parmesan. Set aside.

3. Make kimchi-butter sauce: In the pasta pot or a clean pan, heat the tablespoon of olive oil and the butter over a medium heat. Add the garlic and sauté for 30 seconds, being careful not to brown. Stir in the kimchi and cook for 1–2 minutes, allowing flavours to mingle. Add some kimchi brine for brightness, if desired.

4. Toss the pasta: Return the drained pasta to the pot. Add a splash of the reserved cooking water and toss until each strand is glossy and coated in sauce. Taste and adjust the seasoning with salt and plenty of black pepper.

5. Serve: Divide the pasta between bowls and sprinkle over the Parmesan crumbs. If you like, garnish with extra kimchi pieces or a drizzle of brine and scatter over some fresh chives or spring onion greens.

Kimchi Jeon (Kimchi Pancakes) 김치전

VEGETARIAN / VEGAN OPTION

Makes 2–3 pancakes in a 24–26cm (9½ × 10in) pan

FOR THE CHO-GANJANG (DIPPING SAUCE)

2 tbsp light soy sauce or tamari
1 tbsp rice vinegar
1 tbsp water
½ tsp sesame oil (optional)
Pinch of gochugaru, or ¼–½ fresh chilli, finely sliced
½ tsp toasted sesame seeds

FOR ULTRA-CRISPY, LACY-EDGED KIMCHI JEON

70g (2½oz) plain flour
30g (1oz) rice flour (regular)
20g (¾oz) potato starch (or cornflour)
180–200ml (6¼–7fl oz) ice-cold sparkling water
150g (5¼oz) well-fermented kimchi, lightly drained and finely chopped, plus 2–3 tbsp kimchi brine
3–6 tbsp rapeseed or sunflower oil, for frying

OPTIONAL ADD-INS (CHOOSE 1–2)

2 spring onions, finely sliced
½ mild green chilli, deseeded and thinly sliced
60g (2oz) small prawns or squid, chopped and well dried

Kimchi jeon is one of Korea's most beloved rainy-day snacks – quick to mix, deeply savoury and perfect with a glass of cold makgeolli or beer. Heat mellows the sour, well-fermented kimchi and coaxes out toasty, caramelised edges while the centre stays satisfyingly tender.

This recipe provides two versions so you can choose your texture: an ultra-crispy, lacy pancake or a soft, chewy, comforting one. The secret is in the batter mix, and how you balance flours, starches, egg and water and the elements of pan heat and oil can make all the difference.

---

1. Make dipping sauce: In a small bowl, whisk together all the ingredients. Transfer to a small dipping bowl and set aside while you make the pancakes.

---

1. Make batter: In a bowl, whisk together the flours and starch. Pour in 180ml (6¼fl oz) sparkling water and whisk until smooth, aiming for single-cream consistency.

2. Add kimchi: Stir in the chopped kimchi and its brine, plus any add-ins. Check the consistency again. If the batter feels too runny, whisk in 1–2 teaspoons of flour/starch. If too stiff, add 1–2 teaspoons of sparkling water.

3. Heat pan: Heat a wide frying pan over medium-high heat for 2–3 minutes. Add 2–3 tablespoons of the oil and let it come to temperature. When it shimmers, it's ready to cook in.

4. Pour batter: Pour in 150–180ml (5¼–6¼fl oz) batter and swirl or spread to the edges of the pan. The pancake should be 2–3mm (⅛in) thick. Drizzle 1–2 teaspoons of oil around the edges for a lacy crisp edge.

5. Fry: Cook for 3–4 minutes undisturbed, until the underside is golden and the edges are frilly. Turn the pancake over confidently, and cook the other side for 2–3 minutes. Add a teaspoon of oil if the pan looks dry. Transfer the pancake to a cooling rack or chopping board. Cook the remaining batter in the same way, adding more oil as needed.

6. Rest and serve: Rest the final pancake for 1 minute, cut into wedges and serve warm with the dipping sauce.

FOR SOFT AND CHEWY,
COMFORT-STYLE KIMCHI JEON

100g (3½oz) plain flour
20g (¾oz) glutinous rice flour
160–180ml (5¾–6¼fl oz) room-temperature water
1 egg, lightly beaten
150g (5¼oz) well-fermented kimchi, lightly drained and finely chopped, plus 2–3 tbsp kimchi brine
3–6 tbsp rapeseed or sunflower oil, for frying

OPTIONAL ADD-INS
(CHOOSE 1–2)

2 spring onions, finely sliced
½ mild green chilli, deseeded and thinly sliced
60g (2oz) small prawns or squid, chopped and well dried

Troubleshooting

- Soggy, pale: pan not hot enough; batter too thick; not enough oil.
- Burnt outside, uncooked inside: heat too high; pancake too thick (crispy style).
- Breaks on flipping: not set enough; use wider spatula; add an egg to the batter mix for extra cohesion.
- Too sour: add 1 teaspoon of sugar or some sliced onion; pair with a sweeter dipping sauce.
- No lacey edges on the crispy version: add more ice-cold sparkling water to the batter; drizzle oil around rim.

1. Make batter: In a small bowl, whisk together the flours with 160ml (5¾fl oz) water until smooth. Beat in the egg. Aim for double-cream consistency.

2. Add kimchi: Fold in the chopped kimchi and its brine, plus any add-ins. Check the consistency again. If the batter feels too runny, whisk in 1–2 teaspoons of plain or glutinous rice flour. If too stiff, add 1–2 teaspoons of water.

3. Heat pan: Warm a wide frying pan over medium heat and add 1½–2 tablespoons of oil.

4. Pour batter: Pour 200ml (7fl oz) batter into the pan and swirl or spread to the edges. The pancake should be 5–7mm (¼in) thick.

5. Fry: Cook 4–5 minutes until golden underneath and the edges are set. Flip and cook for 3–4 minutes more. Transfer the pancake to a cooling rack or chopping board. Cook the remaining batter in the same way, adding more oil as needed.

6. Rest and serve: Briefly rest the final pancake for 30–60 seconds, then cut the pancakes into wedges and serve warm with the dipping sauce alongside.

Kimmy's Notes

- **Make ahead:** Batter keeps for 4 hours in the fridge. Keep the crispy version very cold.
- **Leftovers:** Cooked pancakes can be refrigerated for up to 2 days.
- **Reheating:** Re-crisp the crispy version in a pan with 1–2 teaspoons of oil; reheat the soft version in a dry pan or 170°C/150°C Fan/325°F/Gas 3 oven.

Cauliflower & Kimchi Cheese

Serves 2

FOR THE CAULIFLOWER

1 large head cauliflower (about 900g/2lb), cut into medium florets
2 tbsp olive oil

FOR THE CHEESE SAUCE

30g (1oz) unsalted butter
30g (1oz) plain flour
500ml (17½fl oz) whole milk, warmed
100g (3½oz) mature Cheddar, grated
50g (1¾oz) Gruyère or mozzarella, grated
1 tsp Dijon mustard
100g (3½oz) well-fermented kimchi, drained and finely chopped
15g (½oz) panko breadcrumbs (optional)
Sea salt, black pepper and white pepper
Fresh chives or parsley, finely chopped, to garnish

~~~~~~~~

A British classic meets Korean tang. Roasted cauliflower is cloaked in a creamy cheese sauce laced with well-aged kimchi, baked until bubbling and golden. The kimchi cuts through richness with its sour-spicy edge, turning comfort food into something sharper and more dynamic. Aim for kimchi aged 4–8 weeks, bold enough to stand up to strong cheeses. The result is indulgent yet balanced – a dish that reinvents Sunday lunch or makes a vegetarian centrepiece on its own

~~~~~~~~

1. Roast cauliflower: Preheat oven to 200°C/180°C Fan/400°F/Gas 6). Toss the florets with olive oil, salt and black pepper, then spread in a single layer on a roasting tray. Roast for 25–30 minutes, turning halfway, until golden at the edges and tender.

2. Make cheese sauce: In a saucepan over a medium heat, melt the butter. Add the flour and whisk for 1–2 minutes to form a smooth roux. Gradually whisk in the warm milk, a little at a time, to make the sauce. Cook for 3–4 minutes until smooth and slightly thickened. Remove from the heat and stir in the grated cheeses, Dijon mustard and chopped kimchi. Taste and season lightly with salt and white pepper – remember both the cheese and kimchi add salt.

3. Assemble and bake: Reduce the oven to 190°C/170°C Fan/375°F/Gas 5. Transfer the roasted cauliflower into an ovenproof dish. Pour the kimchi-cheese sauce evenly over florets. Sprinkle with panko breadcrumbs, if using, and bake for 15–20 minutes until bubbling and golden on top.

4. Serve: Scatter with fresh chives or parsley and serve.

~~~~~~~~

Well-fermented Kimchi Risotto with Roasted Squash

VEGAN

Serves 2

150g (5¼oz) butternut squash or pumpkin, peeled and cubed (about 2cm/¾in pieces)
1 tbsp olive oil, plus extra for roasting
15g (½oz) butter, or 1 tbsp olive oil
1 small onion, finely chopped
100g (3½oz) well-fermented kimchi (3–6+ weeks), finely chopped, plus 1 tbsp kimchi brine (optional)
150g (5¼oz) Arborio rice
500ml (17½fl oz) hot vegetable stock
2 tbsp grated Parmesan, or vegetarian hard cheese, or vegan alternative
1 tsp toasted sesame oil
Sea salt and black pepper
Chopped fresh chives or thin strips of roasted seaweed, to garnish

This risotto is a marriage of Italian comfort and Korean fermentation, where creamy arborio rice meets the bold tang of aged kimchi. Using kimchi that has been fermenting for at least 3 weeks (ideally closer to 6 weeks) brings deep umami, a complex sourness and a subtle funk that balances beautifully with the natural sweetness of roasted squash or pumpkin. A spoonful of kimchi brine intensifies the tang, and a drizzle of toasted sesame oil ties it all back to Korean tradition. Finished with Parmesan and fresh garnishes, this risotto is both rustic and refined. It's a warming one-pot meal that celebrates the transformative power of fermentation and the richness of seasonal vegetables.

1. Roast squash: Preheat the oven to 200°C/180°C Fan/400°F/Gas 6. Toss the squash cubes with a little olive oil, salt and pepper. Spread on a tray and roast for 25–30 minutes, until golden and tender. Set aside.

2. Sauté aromatics: In a medium pan, heat the olive oil and butter over a medium heat. Add the onion and cook, stirring regularly, for 3–4 minutes until soft and translucent. Stir in the kimchi and cook for 3–4 minutes, until fragrant and slightly caramelised.

3. Toast and cook rice: Add the rice and stir for 1 minute to toast lightly. Begin adding hot stock to the rice one ladleful at a time, stirring frequently. Allow each addition to absorb before adding more. Continue adding stock, stirring regularly, for 20–25 minutes, until the rice is creamy but still with a little bite.

4. Combine and season: Stir in the roasted squash and kimchi brine, if you want a little more tang. Cook for another 1–2 minutes. Taste and adjust seasoning with salt and pepper.

5. Finish and serve: Remove from heat. Stir in the Parmesan and drizzle with toasted sesame oil. Divide into bowls and garnish with chives or seaweed strips. Serve immediately.

Kimchi Jjigae with Mushrooms & Tofu

VEGAN OPTION

Serves 3–4

2 tbsp vegetable oil
100g (3½oz) onion, thinly sliced
30g (1oz) garlic, grated
15g (½oz) ginger, grated
200g (7oz) well-fermented kimchi (3–6+ weeks), roughly chopped, plus 3–5 tbsp kimchi brine
15g (½oz) gochugaru (optional)
200g (7oz) mixed mushrooms such as shiitake, chestnut or button, sliced
400ml (14fl oz) vegetable or anchovy stock
1 tbsp soy sauce or tamari
200g (7oz) firm tofu, cut into 2cm (¾in) cubes
2 tsp toasted sesame oil
Sea salt, to taste
40g (1½oz) spring onions, sliced diagonally, to garnish
5g (⅛oz) toasted sesame seeds, to garnish

Kimchi jjigae is a dish that carries history in every spoonful. It's more than a stew – it's a way of giving new life to kimchi that has gone far beyond its raw stage, developing layers of tanginess and depth after 3 weeks or more. In Korea, when kimchi becomes too sour to eat fresh, it often finds its destiny in a pot of bubbling jjigae. This recipe highlights the sharpness of aged kimchi, softened and balanced by the mellow creaminess of tofu and the earthy notes of mushrooms. Unlike a quick soup, this is a slow-simmered dish that draws out flavour from every ingredient. The onion, garlic and ginger form a fragrant base; kimchi caramelises to release its sour-sweet aroma; mushrooms contribute forest-like richness; and tofu quietly absorbs it all. Finished with sesame oil and spring onions, the stew is bold, warming and deeply restorative. Paired with steamed rice and extra kimchi, it makes a complete meal that satisfies body and soul.

1. Create base: Heat the oil in a medium, heavy pot over a medium heat. Add the onion and cook for 3–4 minutes until softened and translucent. Stir in the garlic and ginger and cook for 30 seconds until fragrant.

2. Cook kimchi and mushrooms: Add the aged kimchi and gochugaru, if you want extra heat. Stir and cook for 3–4 minutes until the kimchi caramelises and releases its aroma. Add the mushrooms and cook for 2–3 minutes until they shrink and release their juices.

3. Simmer broth: Pour in the stock, stirring well. Add soy sauce and kimchi brine to taste. Bring to a boil, then reduce the heat and simmer gently for 10 minutes to deepen flavour.

4. Add tofu and finish cooking: Gently stir in the cubed tofu, simmering for 8–10 minutes so it absorbs the broth. Taste and adjust with salt or add a splash more soy sauce or kimchi brine for depth.

5. Garnish and serve: Turn off the heat and stir in the sesame oil. Ladle into bowls, scatter spring onions on top as well as the sesame seeds, if using, and serve immediately with steamed rice.

Pork Belly & Well-fermented Kimchi Stir-fry

Serves 2–3

300g (10½oz) pork belly, skin removed, thinly sliced
1 tbsp vegetable oil
30g (1oz) garlic, thinly sliced
30g (1oz) ginger, grated
1 small onion, thinly sliced
200g (7oz) well-fermented kimchi, coarsely chopped, plus 1 tbsp kimchi brine (optional)
10g (⅓oz) light brown sugar
1 tsp toasted sesame oil
Sea salt and black pepper
20g (¾oz) spring onions, sliced diagonally, to garnish
10g (⅓oz) toasted sesame seeds, to garnish

Few dishes capture the essence of comfort food in Korea like pork belly stir-fried with well-aged kimchi. The beauty of this dish lies in the balance between rich, savoury pork and the sharp tang of kimchi that has fermented for at least 3 weeks. As the kimchi sizzles in the pork fat, its flavours deepen, transforming sourness into a smoky-sweet intensity that clings to every bite of meat.

It is quick to prepare but delivers layers of flavour that taste as though they have taken hours. The pork belly provides crisp edges and melting tenderness, while the kimchi acts as both vegetable and sauce. A hint of soy and sweetness rounds out the profile, and a drizzle of sesame oil at the end lifts it into something irresistible. Served with steamed rice or lettuce wraps, it's a dish that satisfies on every level.

1. Render pork belly: Place the sliced pork belly into a large skillet over medium heat. Allow the fat to slowly render, stirring occasionally, until the meat turns golden brown and crisp at the edges, which will take 8–10 minutes. Use a slotted spoon to remove the pork to a plate, leaving the flavourful fat in the pan.

2. Sauté aromatics: If the pan looks a little dry, add the oil. Add the garlic, ginger and onion. Sauté for 3–4 minutes until the onion turns translucent and the mixture is fragrant.

3. Cook kimchi: Stir in the kimchi and cook for 5–7 minutes, letting it caramelise slightly.

4. Make sauce and combine: Return the pork belly to the pan. Drizzle in the kimchi brine (if using) and sprinkle over the brown sugar. Toss everything together, coating each piece of pork and kimchi. Cook for another 2 minutes to let the flavours meld and the sauce thicken slightly.

5. Finish and serve: Turn off the heat. Stir in the toasted sesame oil, then taste and adjust the seasoning with salt and pepper, or add a dash more soy sauce, if you like. Transfer to a platter and scatter the spring onions and sesame seeds on top.

Kimchi 'Nduja Pasta

Serves 2–3

200g (7oz) dried pasta (spaghetti, linguine, or casarecce work well)
1 tbsp olive oil, plus extra for drizzling
½ onion, finely chopped
20g (¾oz) garlic, thinly sliced
75g (2½oz) 'nduja (Calabrian spreadable sausage)
150g (5¼oz) well-fermented kimchi (3–6+ weeks), roughly chopped, plus 2 tbsp kimchi brine (optional)
3 tbsp double cream or crème fraîche (optional)
Sea salt and black pepper
10g (⅓oz) fresh parsley, chopped, to garnish
30g (1oz) Parmesan, grated, plus extra to serve
2 tsp extra virgin olive oil, to serve

This dish is a bold meeting of two fermentation traditions: southern Italy's spicy, spreadable 'nduja and Korea's tangy, umami-rich kimchi. Both ingredients are deeply flavourful, fiery and complex, and when combined they create a pasta sauce that is robust yet comforting. The 'nduja melts into the pan, releasing chilli oils and smoky depth, while the aged kimchi contributes acidity and funk, cutting through the richness. The result is a sauce that clings to the pasta, at once spicy, creamy and tangy.

This is a recipe that feels indulgent enough for a dinner party but quick enough for a weeknight. This is fusion at its best: simple, satisfying and deeply memorable.

1. Cook pasta: Bring a large pot of salted water to the boil over a high heat. Add the dried pasta, reduce the heat to medium and cook until just al dente, usually 8–10 minutes. Reserve 100ml (3½fl oz) of the cooking water, then drain in a colander. Toss the pasta with a drizzle of olive oil to prevent it sticking together, then set aside.

2. Prepare aromatics: While the pasta is cooking, heat the olive oil in a large skillet over a medium heat. Add the onion and sauté for 3–4 minutes until softened and lightly golden. Stir in the garlic and cook for 30 seconds until fragrant.

3. Melt 'nduja: Add the 'nduja, breaking it down with a spoon. Let it cook for 1–2 minutes until it releases its spicy oils and turns the mixture glossy and red.

4. Add kimchi: Stir in the chopped kimchi and cook for 2–3 minutes until softened and slightly caramelised. Add the kimchi brine at this stage if you would like extra tang.

5. Make sauce: Pour in the reserved pasta water and stir well to emulsify. Add the cream or crème fraiche, if using, and simmer gently for 1 minute until silky.

6. Toss pasta: Add the drained pasta directly to the skillet. Toss thoroughly until every strand is coated. Taste and then season with salt, if needed, as the 'nduja and kimchi are already quite salty, and black pepper.

7. Finish and serve: Divide into warm bowls. Sprinkle with parsley and Parmesan, drizzle with the extra virgin olive oil, and serve immediately, with extra Parmesan on the side.

Kimchi & Spinach Stuffed Flatbreads

Makes 4–6 flatbreads

FOR THE DOUGH

300g (10½oz) plain flour, plus extra for dusting
½ tsp fine salt
150g (5¼oz) Greek yoghurt
1 tbsp olive oil

FOR THE FILLING

1 tbsp vegetable oil
150g (5¼oz) well-fermented kimchi, finely chopped
100g (3½oz) fresh spinach, washed, stems removed
100g (3½oz) mozzarella, shredded
Sea salt and black pepper

FOR COOKING AND SERVING

1 tbsp oil or ghee
Yoghurt raita or kimchi brine, for dipping

These stuffed flatbreads are a perfect marriage of soft, chewy dough and a bold, savoury filling that brings together the tang of aged kimchi, the freshness of spinach and the creamy pull of melted cheese. The dough requires no yeast or long proving, making it an ideal introduction to flatbreads for home cooks. The technique of stuffing and rolling the dough creates pockets of flavour that burst with each bite, and the charred exterior from the skillet adds a rustic smokiness. They also freeze beautifully, making them a practical batch-cooking option.

---

1. Make dough: In a large bowl, combine the flour and salt. Add the yoghurt and olive oil, stirring until just combined. Add water gradually, 1 tablespoon at a time, until a soft, slightly sticky dough forms. Knead on a floured surface for 5 minutes until smooth and elastic. Cover with a damp tea towel and let it rest on the work surface for 20 minutes.

2. Prepare filling: Heat the oil in a skillet over a medium heat. Add the chopped kimchi and cook for 2–3 minutes until softened and slightly caramelised. Stir in the spinach and cook for about 1 minute, until just wilted. Transfer everything to a bowl and let cool slightly, then mix in the mozzarella. Season lightly with salt and pepper, to taste.

3. Assemble flatbreads: Divide the rested dough into six equal pieces and roll each into a ball. On a floured surface, roll a ball into a 15cm (6in) circle with a rolling pin. Place 2 tablespoons of filling in the centre, gather the edges to the middle and pinch to seal. Flatten gently, then roll out into an 18cm (7in) disc, working carefully to avoid tearing. Repeat with the remaining dough and filling.

4. Cook flatbreads: Heat a skillet over a medium-high heat and brush lightly with oil or ghee. Cook each flatbread for 2–3 minutes per side until puffed, golden brown and charred in spots. Keep warm under a tea towel while finishing the rest.

5. Serve: Cut into wedges and serve hot with yoghurt raita or extra kimchi brine for dipping.

6. Store: Once cooked, allow flatbreads to cool completely. Wrap individually and freeze. Reheat in a dry skillet for 2–3 minutes per side.

Kimchi & Mature Cheddar Muffins

VEGETARIAN

Makes 12 muffins

250g (8¾oz) plain flour
2 tsp baking powder
½ tsp bicarbonate of soda
½ tsp salt
1 tsp sugar
½ tsp black pepper
100g (3½oz) mature Cheddar, grated, plus 20g (¾oz) for topping
120g (4¼oz) well-fermented kimchi, very well drained and finely chopped
1 spring onion, finely sliced
2 medium eggs, beaten
120ml (4¼fl oz) whole milk
100g (3½oz) Greek yoghurt
80ml (3fl oz) rapeseed oil
1 tsp gochugaru (optional)

These muffins bring together the sharp tang of mature Cheddar and the savoury heat of aged kimchi, baked into golden, fluffy parcels that are equally at home on a brunch table, in a lunchbox or as a grab-and-go snack. The key is to use well-fermented kimchi – well drained and finely chopped, so the texture stays light – and a strong Cheddar that won't disappear into the batter. They bake quickly and freeze beautifully, making them a clever make-ahead option for busy weeks. Serve warm with butter or simply enjoy as they are; the kimchi's umami and the Cheddar's sharpness do most of the work.

1. Preheat and prepare: Heat the oven to 200°C/180°C Fan/400°F/Gas 6. Line a 12-hole muffin tin with paper cases or parchment squares.

2. Mix dry ingredients: In a large bowl, whisk together flour, baking powder, bicarbonate of soda, salt, sugar and black pepper. Stir in the grated Cheddar, kimchi and spring onion so they're coated in the flour (this prevents sinking during baking).

3. Mix wet ingredients: In a separate bowl, whisk together eggs, milk, yoghurt and oil until smooth. If using gochugaru, whisk it into this mixture.

4. Combine: Make a well in the centre of the dry ingredients and pour in the wet mixture. Fold gently with a spatula until just combined. The batter should look slightly lumpy – do not overmix, as this leads to dense muffins.

5. Fill tins: Divide the batter evenly among the muffin cases, filling each about two-thirds full. Sprinkle with the extra grated Cheddar for a golden crust.

6. Bake: Bake for 20–22 minutes in the oven until risen, golden and a skewer inserted in the centre comes out clean. Cool in the tin for 5 minutes before transferring to a wire rack.

7. Serve: Enjoy warm with butter, or alongside soup or salad.

8. Store: Keep in an airtight container for up to 3 days, or freeze individually wrapped muffins for up to 2 months. Reheat from frozen in an oven heated to 180°C/160°C Fan/350°F/Gas 4 for 8–10 minutes.

Kimchi & Egg Fried Rice

VEGETARIAN OPTION

Serves 2

300g (10½oz) cold, cooked short-grain rice (1 day old is best)
3 tbsp vegetable oil
½ small onion, diced
1 garlic clove, grated
100g (3½oz) Spam, ham or bacon, diced (optional)
150g (5¼oz) well-fermented mak or pogi kimchi, finely chopped, plus 2 tbsp kimchi brine
2 tbsp gochujang
1 tbsp soy sauce
1 tsp toasted sesame oil
2 eggs
Sea salt and black pepper

TO GARNISH

Chopped spring onions
Gim (seaweed) strips
Toasted sesame seedss

Kimchi-bokkeumbap (김치볶음밥) is Korea's ultimate one-pan comfort: a frugal, flavour-packed meal born from pantry staples and leftover rice. When kimchi turns pungent, we revive it by stir-frying with day-old rice, a splash of brine and simple seasonings, creating a meal in less than 15 minutes. Originating as a post-war necessity, this dish stretches precious ingredients into a sustaining feast. Today, it fills late-night stalls, home kitchens and trendy cafés alike, always reminding us that the humblest meals can be the most memorable. Adapt it freely – add Spam, cheese or a fried egg – but never stray from the core rule: use aged kimchi and cold rice for that signature tang and chewy bite.

1. Prepare rice: Break up the cold rice with your hands or a fork so the grains separate easily.

2. Cook aromatics: Heat 2 tablespoons of the vegetable oil in a skillet or wok over a medium–high heat. Add the onion and garlic and stir-fry for 2–3 minutes until softened and fragrant. If using diced meat, add now and cook until lightly browned.

3. Stir-fry kimchi: Add the chopped kimchi and its brine. Cook for 2–3 minutes until softened and caramelised at the edges.

4. Add rice and seasonings: Stir in the cold rice, followed by the gochujang and soy sauce. Stir vigorously until the grains are evenly coated. Press down occasionally with the spoon to crisp the rice.

5. Finish: Drizzle with sesame oil and season with salt and pepper, if needed. Toss once more to combine.

6. Cook eggs: In a separate frying pan, heat the remaining 1 tablespoon of oil over a medium heat. Crack in the 2 eggs, and fry for 2–4 minutes until the white are set and the yolk is still runny.

7. Serve: Divide the rice between two bowls. Top each portion with a fried egg and garnish with spring onions, gim strips and sesame seeds.

Steak, Stilton & Kimchi Pasties

Makes 4 pasties

5 tbsp vegetable oil
1 small onion, finely chopped
1 medium potato, peeled and diced into 1cm (½in) cubes
250g (8¾oz) beef steak (rump or sirloin), finely diced
½ tsp gochugaru (optional)
150g (5¼oz) well-fermented kimchi, well drained and roughly chopped
100g (3½oz) Stilton (or other strong blue cheese), crumbled
500g (1lb 2oz) shortcrust pastry
1 egg, beaten, to glaze
Sea salt and black pepper

A bold meeting of worlds: the hearty British pasty filled with Korean fire. Tangy kimchi and sharp blue cheese cut through the richness of tender beef, all wrapped in golden pastry. For best balance, use aged kimchi and drain it well to avoid excess salt. The result is a portable feast that's robust, savoury and just a little rebellious, perfect for picnics, lunchboxes or pub-style suppers. Uncooked pasties can be frozen and just need an extra 10 minutes in the oven to cook through .

1. Preheat oven: Preheat the oven to 200°C/180°C Fan/400°F/Gas 6 and line a baking tray.

2. Prepare filling: Heat the oil in a frying pan over a medium heat and sauté the onion and potato for 5–6 minutes until softened but not browned. Add the diced steak and cook briefly, just until the surface loses its raw colour. Season with salt, pepper and gochugaru, if using. Remove from the heat and let cool slightly.

3. Mix with cheese and kimchi: In a large bowl, combine the cooled steak mixture with the chopped kimchi and crumbled Stilton. Stir gently so the ingredients are evenly distributed without becoming mushy.

4. Prepare pastry: Roll out the pastry to 3–4mm (⅛in) thickness. Tracing around a plate about 18cm (7in) wide, cut the pastry into four circles.

5. Fill and shape pasties: Place a quarter of the filling onto one half of each pastry circle, leaving a border. Brush the edge lightly with beaten egg, fold the pastry over and crimp the edges firmly to seal.

6. Bake: Place the pasties on the baking tray. Brush the tops with beaten egg, then put in the oven to bake for 30–35 minutes, until the pastry is crisp and golden.

7. Cool and serve: Let them rest for 10 minutes before eating to allow the filling to settle. Serve warm or at room temperature.

8. Storage: Freeze unbaked pasties on a tray, then bag them up – they can be baked straight from frozen, adding an extra 10 minutes.

Kimchi Pasta with Gochujang Butter

VEGETARIAN OPTION

serves 2

200g (7oz) dried fusilli pasta
30g (1oz) unsalted butter
1½ tbsp gochujang
2 garlic cloves, thinly sliced
1 small shallot, finely chopped
150g (5¼oz) mid-fermented kimchi, roughly chopped
1 tbsp kimchi juice
2 tbsp olive oil
2 tsp toasted sesame oil
1 tsp toasted sesame seeds
Black pepper

OPTIONAL GARNISHES

Sliced spring onions
Chilli flakes
Grated Parmesan, or vegetarian hard cheese

This is weeknight comfort with a twist. Butter and gochujang melt into a glossy, spicy base, while kimchi adds acidity and bite. Tossed with pasta and finished with sesame oil, every bit of pasta is coated in bold, savoury flavour. A sprinkle of Parmesan or spring onions makes it fusion at its best – familiar yet new. For depth without mushiness, use kimchi that's 2–3 weeks old, when sourness is bright and there is still some texture.

1. Cook pasta: Bring a large pot of salted water to the boil. Add the pasta and cook until just al dente. Reserve 100ml (3½fl oz) of cooking water, then drain the pasta.

2. Make gochujang butter: In a skillet or the empty pasta pot, melt the butter over a medium heat. Stir in the gochujang until smooth. Add the garlic and shallot, and sauté gently for 1–2 minutes until fragrant but not browned.

3. Make sauce: Add the chopped kimchi and its juice to the pan and stir-fry for 2–3 minutes until softened slightly. Add in the olive oil and a splash of pasta water, stirring to emulsify into a silky sauce.

4. Toss pasta: Add the drained pasta back into the pan. Drizzle with sesame oil and season with cracked black pepper. Toss for 1–2 minutes until all the pasta is coated and glossy. Add more pasta water to loosen the sauce, if you like.

5. Serve: Divide between warm bowls. Top with toasted sesame seeds and add garnishes as desired: spring onion, chilli flakes and/or Parmesan.

Vegan Kimchi Mandu
김치만두

VEGAN

Makes 30 dumplings

FOR THE DOUGH

250g (8¾oz) plain flour, plus extra for dusting
Pinch of sea salt
130ml (4½fl oz) water

FOR THE FILLING

360g (13oz) firm tofu
300g (10½oz) beansprouts
75g (2½oz) glass noodles (dangmyeon), soaked, boiled and chopped
825g (1lb 13oz) well-fermented kimchi, squeezed and finely chopped
1 small spring onion, finely chopped
2 tbsp soy sauce
30g (1oz) grated garlic
30g (1oz) gochugaru
1 tbsp perilla oil or sesame oil
Pinch of sugar (optional)
Sea salt and black pepper

FOR THE DIPPING SAUCE

2 tbsp soy sauce
1 tbsp vinegar
1 tbsp water
1 tsp sugar or rice syrup
Pinch of gochugaru

These vegan dumplings are a celebration of texture and flavour: tangy, well-fermented kimchi meets tofu, sprouts and glass noodles, all wrapped in tender homemade dough. They can be steamed, pan-fried or dropped into jjigae (page 162) or jeongol (page 147), making them one of the most versatile and beloved Korean dishes.

1. Make dough: In a large bowl, mix the flour and a pinch of salt. Gradually drizzle in water while stirring until a rough ball forms. Knead the dough on a lightly floured surface for 8–10 minutes until smooth and elastic. Wrap in cling film and rest in the fridge for 1 hour.

2. Prepare filling: Bring a medium pan of water to the boil over a high heat. Blanch the tofu briefly, remove from the pan with a slotted spoon and leave in a colander to drain. When cool enough to handle, squeeze well and finely crumble into a large mixing bowl. Next, blanch the beansprouts for 30–60 seconds. Transfer to the colander and rinse under cold water to stop them cooking further. Squeeze dry, chop finely and add to tofu. Soak the glass noodles (dangmyeon) in warm water for 20–30 minutes until pliable. Drain, then boil for 10–15 minutes until cooked through. Rinse, drain well and chop into short lengths. Finely chop them and add to the mixing bowl. Finally, squeeze the kimchi dry and finely chop before adding to the mixing bowl too.

3. Mix filling: To the bowl with the fillings, add the spring onion and mix well. Add the soy sauce, garlic, gochugaru, perilla or sesame oil, sugar, if using, and salt and pepper, to taste. Mix thoroughly until everything is evenly seasoned.

4. Shape wrappers: After resting, tip the dough out onto a lightly floured work surface and roll into a rope about 2.5cm (1in) thick. Cut into 1.5cm (½in) slices (about 12g/⅓oz each). Roll each slice into a thin 9cm (4in) circle, dusting with flour as needed. Stack with flour or parchment between to prevent sticking.

5. Assemble dumplings: Place 1 tablespoon of filling in the centre of each wrapper. Wet the edges lightly with water, fold the wrapper over and press the edges to seal. Pleat if desired. Avoid overfilling to prevent bursting.

6. Make dipping sauce: In a small bowl, combine all the dipping sauce ingredients and set aside.

7. Freeze (optional): If making ahead or you have made more than you need, arrange uncooked dumplings on a tray, freeze them until solid then transfer to a bag. These can be cooked from frozen, adding 2-3 extra minutes to any of the cooking methods.

8. Cook mandu (choose one):

a. Steam: Place dumplings in a cloth-lined steamer basket over a pan of barely simmering water. Steam for 15 minutes until translucent and tender.
b. Pan fry: Heat a little oil in a non-stick pan over a medium heat. Cook the dumplings for a few minutes until golden on both sides, before adding 2-3 tbsp water and covering with a lid for 3-4 minutes to steam fry.
c. Soup or hotpot: Drop the dumplings into simmering broth. Cook for 5-6 minutes until the wrappers are cooked through.

9. Serve: Arrange the steamed or pan-fried dumplings on a platter and serve with the dipping sauce on the side.

Kimchi Quesadilla

VEGETARIAN

Serves 2

2 large flour tortillas
100g (3½oz) mature Cheddar or Monterey Jack, grated
100g (3½oz) well-fermented napa kimchi, well drained and finely chopped
20g (¾oz) fresh coriander or spring onions, chopped
1 tbsp vegetable oil
60g (2oz) sour cream or natural yoghurt
1 lime, cut into wedges

This is a perfect example of how two comfort food traditions can meet in the middle. Crispy, golden tortillas hug a filling of melty cheese and tangy, spicy kimchi, creating a dish that is at once gooey, crunchy and deeply satisfying. The rich dairy balances the fermented heat of the kimchi, while fresh herbs add brightness. In under 15 minutes, you'll have a snack, light meal or sharing plate that feels indulgent yet easy. Paired with sour cream or yoghurt and a squeeze of lime, it's a bold twist on the classic quesadilla.

1. Assemble quesadillas: Lay a tortilla out on a clean work surface. Sprinkle a quarter of the grated cheese over half of the tortilla, then top with half the kimchi and half the coriander or spring onions. Scatter another quarter of the cheese on top, then fold the empty half over the filling to form a semicircle. Repeat with the other tortilla and the remaining fillings.

2. Cook: Place a large dry skillet or griddle over a medium heat and brush lightly with oil. Slide the folded tortilla into the pan and cook for 2–3 minutes per side, pressing gently with a spatula, until golden brown and crisp, and the cheese has fully melted.

3. Repeat: Transfer the first quesadilla to a board and keep warm under foil. Cook the second tortilla in the same way.

4. Serve: Cut each quesadilla into three or four wedges. Serve hot with sour cream or yoghurt and lime wedges for squeezing over.

Blended Kimchi Sauce Collection

Kimchi is not only eaten on its own. When blended, it becomes a set of versatile sauces that bring spicy, tangy, umami depth to many dishes.

These sauces are simple to make and easy to keep on hand. With a few jars in the refrigerator, you can add the flavour of fermentation to weeknight meals in seconds

Classic Blended Kimchi Sauce

VEGAN

Makes: about 250ml (8¾fl oz)

150g (5¼oz) mid-fermented kimchi, roughly chopped, plus 3 tbsp kimchi brine
2 tbsp vegetable stock or water
1 garlic clove, grated
2 tsp toasted sesame oil
Sea salt and black pepper

Kimmy's Notes

- If your kimchi is very acidic, blend in 1 tbsp plain yoghurt to soften the edges without losing character.

Notes on making and scaling up sauces:

- **Kimchi age:** Mid- to well-fermented kimchi gives the strongest flavour for sauces. Younger kimchi tastes milder and more vegetal.
- **Consistency control:** To thin, add 1–2 tablespoons of water or brine.
  To thicken, simmer gently for 1–2 minutes or chill.
- **Heat adjustment:** Increase or reduce gochugaru by ½–1 teaspoon to taste.
- **Batch size:** For double batches, increase all ingredients proportionally and extend blending time by 30 seconds for a smooth finish.

A smooth, bright sauce that captures the flavour of mid-fermented kimchi in a pourable form. It is excellent as a table sauce, a noodle dressing or a quick base for marinades.

1. **Blend:** Add kimchi, kimchi brine, stock or water and garlic to a blender. Blend until completely smooth. Scrape down the sides and blend again for a fine texture.

2. **Season:** Stir in the toasted sesame oil. Taste and season with salt and pepper.

3. **Store:** Transfer to a clean jar. Chill for 30 minutes to let flavours settle. Refrigerate for up to 7 days. If it thickens, loosen with 1–2 teaspoons of water.

Serving Suggestions

- Spoon over rice bowls and fried eggs.
- Toss with cold noodles.
- Drizzle on grilled vegetables.
- Use as a quick marinade for tofu or chicken.

Spicy, Sweet Kimchi Glaze

VEGETARIAN

Makes: about 220ml (7¾fl oz)

120g (4¼oz) well-fermented kimchi, chopped, plus 1½ tbsp kimchi brine
2 tbsp light soy sauce
1½ tbsp honey or sugar
2 tsp rice vinegar
15g (½oz) gochugaru (optional)
2 tsp toasted sesame oil

Kimmy's Notes

- For a deeper lacquer, reduce the glaze for 1 more minute and apply two thin coats to your meat, fish or veg during cooking.

A glossy, sticky glaze that balances heat, salt and sweetness. It clings beautifully to roasted vegetables, grilled meats and tofu.

1. **Blend:** Blend the kimchi, kimchi brine, soy sauce, honey or sugar, rice vinegar and gochugaru, if using, until smooth.

2. **Cook:** Pour into a saucepan and simmer gently for 3-4 minutes, stirring, until the sauce is slightly thickened and glossy. Remove from the heat and stir in toasted sesame oil. Cool to room temperature.

3. **Store:** Pour into a clean jar or bottle and keep in the fridge. Refrigerate for up to 5 days. If it thickens, loosen with 1-2 teaspoons of water.

Serving Suggestions

- Brush on aubergine, squash or cauliflower before roasting.
- Glaze chicken wings or salmon in the final minutes of cooking.
- Drizzle over grain bowls.

Kimchi Butter

VEGETARIAN

Makes: about 200g (7oz)

100g (3½oz) kimchi, well drained and very finely minced or blended
100g (3½oz) unsalted butter, softened
10g (⅓oz) fresh parsley, finely chopped
2 garlic cloves, grated
Sea salt and black pepper

Serving Suggestions

- Toss through steamed greens or warm noodles.
- Spread on toasted sourdough.

Soft butter carries kimchi's heat and tang beautifully, making it an excellent spread or finishing butter to melt onto steaks, vegetables or noodles.

1. **Mix:** Combine the minced kimchi, softened butter, parsley and garlic in a bowl with a fork or wooden spoon. Keep mixing until uniform. Taste, and season lightly with salt and pepper.

2. **Shape:** Spoon onto parchment and roll into a tight log. Chill until firm, then slice into discs.

3. **Store:** Refrigerate for upto 7 days or freeze for up to 3 months. Separate discs with small pieces of parchment for easy handling.

KIMCHI TROUBLESHOOTING – PROBLEMS, REASONS & FIXES

Kimchi is alive and that means it can sometimes surprise you. If you're new to fermentation, don't worry when things don't look or taste exactly as you expected. Most changes are completely normal, and when something goes a little wrong, there's usually an easy way to fix it.

Too Salty

If your kimchi tastes overly salty, it usually means the vegetables stayed in the brine for too long, or you used salted seafood without adjusting the balance of added salt. The cabbage should bend easily but still have some strength, not collapse.

Quick Fix: After brining, rinse the vegetables gently in cold water to wash away surface salt. If fermentation has already started, mix in some fresh, unsalted vegetables like radish sticks or extra napa leaves to absorb the excess.
Next Time: Trust texture more than numbers. Stop brining as soon as the leaves are pliable but still crisp and remember that fish sauce or saeujeot also adds salt, so adjust the seasoning paste accordingly.

Kimmy's Tip

- How Salty Should the Brine Be? Salty Enough to Make a Face.
When I was little, my grandmother would hand me a spoonful of fresh kimchi brine and say, 'If it doesn't make you pull a face, it isn't salty enough. That shocking saltiness is what protects the cabbage and makes sure the good fermentation begins. Don't panic – the cabbage will be rinsed, the seasoning will balance it, and the souring will soften it all. If your finished kimchi still feels too salty, give it a gentle rinse or fold in some fresh, unsalted vegetables.

Too Soft or Limp

Kimchi should stay crunchy, but sometimes it gets soft. This happens if the cabbage was brined too long or if it ferments in a hot place.

Quick Fix: Don't throw it away – use softer kimchi in cooking, like kimchi stew (jjigae), fried rice or dumplings.
Next Time: Brine for a shorter time and keep your jar in a cooler spot at home, or transfer to the fridge sooner.

Not Fermenting

If your kimchi isn't bubbling or turning tangy, the 'good bacteria' aren't active yet. This can happen when it's too cold or the brine is too salty.

Quick Fix: Move the jar to a warmer place, around 18–22°C (65–70°F) (a normal room temperature). If it's too salty, remove some of the brine and top up with filtered water. Be careful not to dilute the concentration too far the other way.
Next Time: Measure the salt carefully and keep the jar at a steady room temperature (18–22°C/65–70°F), avoiding large fluctuations in temperature.

Fermenting Too Fast

If your kimchi goes sour too quickly, it usually means your kitchen is very warm, or you added a lot of fruit or sugar.

Quick Fix: Put the jar in the fridge as soon as the flavour feels right for you.
Next Time: Use less sugar or fruit, and let the jar sit in the coolest part of your kitchen.

Strange Smell

Kimchi should smell fresh, sour and appetising. A strong cheesy smell can still be safe (best used in cooking), but rotten or chemical-like smells mean it should be thrown away.
Quick Fix: If the smell is just tangy or strong, cook with it. If it smells rotten or like nail polish remover, discard it.
Next Time: Always use clean jars and utensils, and don't add too much seafood paste.

White Film on Top

A thin white layer is usually yeast, not mould. It's harmless, but it can make flavours less pleasant.

Quick Fix: Gently scoop it off and press the vegetables back under the liquid.
Next Time: Pack the jar tightly so fewer air pockets remain, and make sure everything is coated in paste or brine.

Timing and Flavour

Kimchi changes every day – and that's part of the fun! Here's a simple guide for when to eat it:

- **Day 0:** Fresh and crunchy, like salad.
- **Days 1–3:** A little tangy, bubbly, crisp.
- **Days 4–7:** Juicy and balanced – classic table kimchi.
- **Weeks 2–3:** Softer and sourer – great for stews and fried rice.
- **1–2 months:** Very sour and rich – best for long-cooked dishes.

Every jar of kimchi is teaching you something. Don't be afraid of mistakes. They're just part of learning. Keep notes about how much salt you used, how long you left it out, and what the flavour was like each day. Soon, you'll start to trust your senses and know exactly when your kimchi is ready, just the way you like it.

GLOSSARY OF KOREAN INGREDIENTS & TERMS

Korean food is built on layers of flavour – salt, spice, fermentation, herbs and grains. Many ingredients carry centuries of history and cultural meaning. This glossary offers a clear guide to help you recognise and use them with confidence.

Fermentation & Seasoning Staples

Gochugaru (고춧가루) – Korean red chilli flakes, coarse or fine; fruity, mildly smoky and with balanced heat.

Gochujang (고추장) – A fermented chilli paste traditionally made with glutinous rice (chapssal), fermented soybeans, barley malt powder/extract (yeotgireum) and chilli; thick, sweet-spicy and umami.

Doenjang (된장) – Fermented soybean paste, earthy and salty, the backbone of soups and stews.

Cheonggukjang (청국장) – A fast-fermented soybean paste with a strong aroma; richer, funkier and often used in hearty jjigae.

Meju (메주) – Dried, fermented soybean blocks, used to make soy sauce and doenjang.

Meju garu (메주가루) – Powdered dried meju blocks; used in making gochujang and sometimes for quicker versions of doenjang.

Aekjeot (액젓) – Korean fish sauce, most often from anchovies; briny, salty and essential for kimchi.

Saeujeot (새우젓) – Tiny salted shrimp; sharp and salty, used in kimchi.

Jeotgal (젓갈) – The broader category of salted, fermented seafood, including saeujeot, aekjeot and others.

Yeotgireum (엿기름) – Barley malt, sprouted barley, soaked to make malt water (yeotgireum-mul), used for fermenting drinks like sikhye and for pastes.

Ganjang (간장) – Korean soy sauce; types include:
- Guk-ganjang (국간장): Clear, pale, very salty; brewed only from soybeans and brine.
- Jin-ganjang (진간장): Darker, usually blended or commercially brewed, often with wheat.
- Makjang (막장) – It's a mixed condiment (doenjang + gochujang + aromatics) eaten fresh, usually as a dipping sauce.
- Ssamjang (쌈장) – A dipping paste of gochujang, doenjang, garlic and sesame oil.

Vegetables, Fruits & Herbs

Baechu (배추) – Napa cabbage, the base of classic kimchi.

Mu (무) – Korean white radish; firm, crisp and peppery.

Chonggakmu (총각무) – 'Ponytail' radish with leaves attached.

Yeolmu (열무) – Young summer radish greens, refreshing in chilled soups.

Bomdong (봄동) – Spring cabbage, delicate and perfect for fresh kimchi.

Oi (오이) – Cucumber, often stuffed as oi-sobagi kimchi.

Pa (파) – Korean spring onion; more pungent and aromatic than Western spring onions.

Buchu (부추) – Garlic chives, grassy and garlicky.

Kkaennip (깻잎) – Perilla leaves, minty and similar in appearance to Japanese shiso, but distinct in flavour. Grassy and used in wraps or pickles.

Maneul (마늘) – Garlic, foundational to Korean flavour.

Saenggang (생강) – Fresh ginger, warming and balancing.

Minari (미나리) – Korean water celery, bright and peppery.

Gam (감) – Persimmon, eaten fresh or dried (gotgam).

Bae (배) – Korean pear, sweet and crisp; used in marinades and kimchi paste.

Cheongyang gochu (청양고추) – A popular Korean chilli pepper, smaller and much hotter than everyday Korean green chillies.

Grains, Beans & Sweeteners

Ssal (쌀) – Rice, the foundation of Korean meals.
Mepssal (멥쌀) – Non-glutinous, everyday rice.
Chapssal (찹쌀) – Glutinous rice, used in rice cakes and kimchi paste.
Bap (밥) – Cooked rice, always served warm and plain.
Japgokbap (잡곡밥) – Mixed grain rice.
Dangmyeon (당면) – Sweet potato starch noodles, used in japchae.
Kkae (깨) – Sesame seeds, usually toasted.
Chamgireum (참기름) – Korean toasted sesame oil, nutty and aromatic.
Mulyeot (물엿) – Starch syrup, mild and glossy.
Maesil-cheong (매실청) – Green plum syrup, sweet-tart and digestive.
Nurungji (누룽지) – Crispy scorched rice from the bottom of the pot, eaten as a snack or steeped in hot water.

Seaweed & Pantry Staples

Gim (김) – Seaweed sheets, often roasted with sesame oil and salt.
Miyeok (미역) – Wakame seaweed, used in soups like miyeok-guk.
Dashima (다시마) – Kelp, for stocks and broths.
Myeolchi (멸치) – Dried anchovies, simmered for broth.
Jangajji (장아찌) – Vegetables preserved in soy sauce, vinegar or pastes; primarily pickled, not deeply fermented.
Kkaennip jangajji (깻잎 장아찌) – Soy-brined perilla leaves.

Kimchi & Ferments

Kimchi (김치) – Fermented vegetables, Korea's most iconic dish.
Baechu-kimchi (배추김치) – Whole napa cabbage kimchi.
Mak-kimchi (막김치) – Chopped 'everyday' kimchi.
Kkakdugi (깍두기) – Cubed radish kimchi.
Chonggak-kimchi (총각김치) – Whole ponytail radish kimchi.
Oi-sobagi (오이소박이) – Stuffed cucumber kimchi.
Baek-kimchi (백김치) – White, non-spicy napa kimchi.
Dongchimi (동치미) – Clear radish water kimchi.
Nabak-kimchi (나박김치) – Pink-tinged water kimchi with cabbage and radish.
Gat-kimchi (갓김치) – Mustard leaf kimchi.

Dishes & Meals

Bibimbap (비빔밥) – Mixed rice bowl with vegetables, egg, meat and gochujang.
Kimchi bokkeumbap (김치볶음밥) – Fried rice with aged kimchi.
Kimchi jjigae (김치찌개) – Kimchi stew, often with pork or tofu.
Budae jjigae (부대찌개) – 'Army base stew', with Spam, sausages, noodles and kimchi.
Jeon (전) – Savoury pancakes.
Pajeon (파전) – Spring onion pancakes.
Naengmyeon (냉면) – Cold buckwheat noodles in chilled broth.
Kimchi-mari guksu (김치말이국수) – Cold noodles in kimchi brine.
Sujebi (수제비) – Hand-torn noodle soup.
Kalguksu (칼국수) – Knife-cut noodle soup.
Ssam (쌈) – Leaf wraps filled with rice, meat and condiments.

Tools & Techniques

Onggi (옹기) – Traditional clay fermentation jars.
Hangari (항아리) – Large pottery vessels for pastes and sauces.
Jeorim (절임) – Salting stage in kimchi-making.
Juk (죽) – Rice porridge, sometimes used in kimchi paste.
Yangnyeom (양념) – Seasoning or marinade.
Gamchil-mat (감칠맛) – Umami; a savoury depth of flavour. A modern loanword but now common in Korean food culture.

INDEX

Note: page numbers in **bold** refer to illustrations.

acidity levels 35
aerobic conditions 29
alcohol 29
anaerobic conditions 28, 29
anchovy 22–3, 138
anchovy fish sauce 11, 17, 21, 23, 48
apple 22, 31
    asparagus-chive kimchi 92–3
    chopped oi kimchi 97
    dongchimi 72–3
    kale & sweet potato kimchi 110–11
    mak kimchi 62–3, **64–5**
    oi-sobagi 76–7
    pa kimchi 66, **67**
    pogi kimchi 59–60, **61**
    pumpkin & sage kimchi 114
    yeolmu kimchi 74–5
Asian pear
    chopped oi kimchi 97
    kale & sweet potato kimchi 110–11
    pumpkin & sage kimchi 114
    wild garlic kimchi 88–9
asparagus-chive kimchi 92–3
aubergine 23
    gaji kimchi 80–1
autumnal kimchi 108–15
avocado
    kimchi avocado toast 126, **127**
    kimchi summer rolls **128**, 129
    kimchi tofu scramble on toast 130, **131**

bacon, kimchi & egg fried rice **172**, 173
bacteria, lactic acid 28–9, 32, 34–6, 38, 47, 49
baechu gogaengi kimchi 23
baechu (Korean napa cabbage) kimchi 12, 30, 43
baek kimchi 54, **55**, 69
baked bean
    budae jjigae 138, **139**
    kimchi baked beans on sourdough 152, **153**
bap-sang 18
beef, steak, Stilton & kimchi pasties 174, **175**
beetroot
    beetroot & pear kimchi 109
    beetroot kimchi 17
bindaetteok, kimchi 150, **151**
binding agents 49
birth of kimchi 16–17
bossam (boiled pork) kimchi 22
breadcrumbs, Parmesan 154, **155**
broccoli kimchi 87
Brussels sprout kimchi 17
    sobagi-style 120
buchu (garlic chives) kimchi 68
budae jjigae (army stew) 138, **139**
butter
    gochujang butter 176, **177**
    kimchi & butter pasta with Parmesan crumbs 154, **155**
    kimchi butter 183

cabbage 12–13, 16–18, 22–3, 31–4
    cut of the 11, 19, 30, 54
    how to tell if it is properly salted 41–2
    rinsing and draining 12
    salting 12, 41–2
    shredded 30
    see also napa cabbage; Savoy cabbage kimchi
cabbage (red), kimchi summer rolls **128**, 129

carbon dioxide 29, 32, 35
carrot
    baek kimchi 69
    buchu kimchi 68
    budae jjigae 138, **139**
    gaji kimchi 80–1
    ginger & pear kimchi 112, **113**
    kimchi summer rolls **128**, 129
    Morkovcha-inspired carrot kimchi 94, **95**
    oi-sobagi 76–7
cauliflower & kimchi cheese 159
celeriac
    celeriac kimchi 118, **119**
    winter root vegetable kimchi 122, **123**
cheese
    budae jjigae 138, **139**
    cauliflower & kimchi cheese 159
    cheese sauce 159
    kimchi & cheese empanadas 144–5
    kimchi & mature Cheddar muffins 170, **171**
    kimchi & potato gratin 140, **141**
    kimchi & spinach stuffed flatbreads 168, **169**
    kimchi grilled cheese sandwich 136, **137**
    kimchi mac & cheese 142, **143**
    kimchi quesadilla 180, **181**
    steak, Stilton & kimchi pasties 174, **175**
    see also Parmesan
chilli 13, 23, 32
    green 72–3, 156–8
    problems with 46
    red 97, 98–9
    see also gochugaru
chimchae 16
Chinese cabbage 43
Chinese leaf 43
chive(s) 104, 106, 126, 144–5
cho-ganjang 156–8, **157**
chogochujang sauce **128**, 129
chonggak kimchi 70–1
chopped oi kimchi 97
Chungcheong-do kimchi 22–3
cleanliness 51
coriander (fresh)
    empanadas 144–5
    quesadilla 180, **181**
    summer herb kimchi 101
    summer rolls **128**, 129
coriander (ground), Morkovcha-inspired carrot kimchi 94, **95**
courgette 23
    courgette ribbon kimchi 106, **107**
    vegan kimchi mandu jeongal 147
craft of kimchi 13, 26–55
cucumber
    cucumber & mint kimchi 105
    cucumber kimchi 31, 54
    kimchi summer rolls **128**, 129
    kimchi-mari guksu **148**, 149
    oi-sobagi 76–7
    see also Korean cucumber

daikon 12, 20, 43–5
    baek kimchi 69
    broccoli kimchi 87
    Brussels sprout kimchi 120
    dongchimi 72–3
    geotjeori 78–9
    goguma mul kimchi 98–9
    leek & mustard seed kimchi 121
    mak kimchi 62–3, **64–5**
    min-deul-le kimchi 90–1

Savoy cabbage kimchi 115
summer herb kimchi 101
wild garlic kimchi 88–9
yeolmu kimchi 74–5
dandelion (min-deul-le) kimchi 90–1
defining kimchi 12
dill 101, 106
dipping sauces 140, **141**, 147, 150, **151**, 156–8, **157**, 178–9
doenjang 23
dongchimi (light water radish kimchi) 13, 17, 22, 32, 44–5
    recipe 72–3
douchi 30
dumplings *see* mandu

egg
    kimchi & egg fried rice **172**, 173
    kimchi-mari guksu **148**, 149
elements of kimchi 43–50
empanadas, kimchi cheese 144–5
Eumsik Dimibang 16

fennel 109
fermentation 13, 16, 24, 28–37, 124
    burping jars 36–7
    and daikon 44
    day-by-day 34–7, 185
    and garlic 47
    and gochugaru 46
    good/bad signs 37
    and jeotgal 49
    lactic-acid 13, 17, 28–9, 32, 34–6
    mould 28, 29–30
    and radishes 44
    and rice porridge 49
    and salt 38–40, 42
    single-jar 17
    and sugar 31–2
    and temperature 36, 185
    troubleshooting 184–5
    yeast 28, 29
fermentation vessels 52–3
five principles of kimchi 30–1
flatbreads, kimchi & spinach stuffed 168, **169**
flavour 21–4, 31, 37, 49, 185
foundations of kimchi 30
fresh kimchi
    recipes using 124–32
    see also geotjeori
future of kimchi 17

gaji kimchi 80–1
Gangwon-do kimchi 22
ganjang 29, 30
garlic 12, 16, 19, 32, 33, 46–7, 49
garlic chives kimchi 68
garnishes 55
geotjeori (fresh spring kimchi) 17, 22, 31, 54, 86, 124
    recipe 78–9
ginger 12, 16, 19, 32–3, 46–9
    carrot, ginger & pear kimchi 112, **113**
glaze, spicy, sweet kimchi 183
gochugaru (Korean chilli flakes) 11, 12, 19, 21, 23, 30, 33
    definition 45–6
    goun (fine) 45
    gulgeun (coarse) 45
    revolution of 16–17
    taeyangcho variety 46
gochujang 13, 29, 30–1
    budae jjigae 138, **139**
    chogochujang sauce **128**, 129

gochujang butter 176, **177**
stir-fried kimchi udon with greens 132, **133**
goguma mul (purple sweet potato) kimchi 98–9
gratin, kimchi & potato 140, **141**
Greek yoghurt 168, 170
greens with stir-fried kimchi udon 132, **133**
Gyeonggi-do kimchi 22
Gyeongsang 21–2, 23
Gyeongsang-do 21–2
Gyeongsangbuk-do 21–2

ham/spam
    budae jjigae 138, **139**
    kimchi & egg fried rice **172**, 173
Hamgyong-do 23
herb(s), summer herb kimchi 101

imwon gyeongjeji 16

Jang Gye-hyang, Lady 16
jang kimchi 22
jars 10, 16, 32, 36–7, 53
Jeju 23
Jeju-do kimchi 23
Jeolla 23
Jeollabuk-do 21
Jeollanam-do 21
jeon, kimchi jeon (kimchi pancakes) 156–8, **157**
jeotgal (fermented seafood) 16, 17, 21–3, 32, 46–9
    see also saeujeot
Jerusalem artichoke 122
jjigae, kimchi jjigae with mushrooms & tofu 162, **163**
jujube(s) (dried Korean dates) 23, 72–3
juk (rice porridge) 33, 49

kale
    kale & sweet potato kimchi 110–11
    kale kimchi 17
    kimchi & quinoa one-pot stew 135
kelp water alternative 12, 31, 49–50
kimchi brine 33, 35–7, 38, 54
kimchi-mari guksu (noodles in cold kimchi brine) **148**, 149
kimjang (communal making of kimchi) 17, 18–20, 43, 116
kkaennip kimchi 82
kkakdugi 17, 44–5
kohlrabi & nectarine white kimchi 104
Korean cucumber
    chopped oi kimchi 97
    cucumber & mint kimchi 105
    oi-sobagi 76–7
Korean culture 18–20
Korean diaspora 20, 23
Korean jjokpa 66
Korean peninsula 21, 23–4

lactic-acid fermentation 13, 17, 28–9, 32, 34–6
Lactobacillus plantarum 35–6
leek & mustard seed kimchi 121
Leuconostoc mesenteroides 35

mac & cheese, kimchi 142, **143**
maesil-cheong (plum syrup)
    buchu kimchi 68
    chopped oi kimchi 97
    watermelon rind kimchi 100
mak kimchi 30, 51
    kimchi & egg fried rice **172**, 173
    recipe 62–3, **64–5**
mandu (dumplings)
    vegan kimchi mandu 178–9

vegan kimchi mandu jeongal 147
maturity guides 60, 63
microbes 13, 17, 28, 35
    harmful 32, 34, 35, 37, 38, 47, 51
    see also bacteria; specific microbes; yeast
microgreens 126
mid-fermented kimchi (1-3 weeks old), recipes using 134–45, 182
min-deul-le (dandelion) kimchi 90–1
mint
    courgette ribbon kimchi 106, **107**
    cucumber & mint kimchi 105
    kimchi summer rolls **128**, 129
    summer herb kimchi 101
    watermelon rind kimchi 100
miso 13, 20, 29, 30, 31
Morkovcha-inspired carrot kimchi 94, **95**
mould fermentation 28, 29–30
mould formation 32, 37
mu (Korean radish) 43–5
    dongchimi 72–3
    gaji kimchi 80–1
    geotjeori 78–9
    goguma mul kimchi 98–9
    pogi kimchi 59–60, **61**
    yeolmu kimchi 74–5
mu mallaengi (dried shredded radish) kimchi 83
muffins, kimchi & mature Cheddar 170, **171**
mung bean, kimchi bindaetteok 150, **151**
mushroom
    budae jjigae 138, **139**
    kimchi jjigae with mushrooms & tofu 162, **163**
    vegan kimchi mandu jeongal 147
mustard leaves 21, 23
mustard seed &a leek kimchi 121

nabak kimchi 32
napa cabbage 12, 16, 19–20, 23, 30, 43, 58
    baek kimchi 69
    geotjeori 78–9
    kimchi & potato gratin 140, **141**
    kimchi avocado toast 126, **127**
    kimchi grilled cheese sandwich 136, **137**
    kimchi mac & cheese 142, **143**
    kimchi quesadilla 180, **181**
    kimchi summer rolls with chogochujang sauce **128**, 129
    kimchi tofu scramble on toast 130, **131**
    mak kimchi 62–3, **64–5**
    pogi kimchi 59–60, **61**
    preparation 51
    rinsing 51–2
    vegan kimchi mandu jeongal 147
    see also baechu kimchi
'nduja, kimchi 'nduja pasta 166, **167**
nectarine & kohlrabi white kimchi 104
noodles
    budae jjigae 138, **139**
    kimchi summer rolls with chogochujang sauce **128**, 129
    kimchi-mari guksu (noodles in cold kimchi brine) **148**, 149
    stir-fried kimchi udon with greens 132, **133**
    vegan kimchi mandu 178–9
North Korea 23

oi-sobagi 76–7
onggi (clay jars) 16, 32
onion 97
onion (red) 94, 97
oral tradition 19
oysters 17, 21, 48

pa kimchi 66, **67**
pancakes
    kimchi bindaetteok 150, **151**
    kimchi jeon (kimchi pancakes) 156–8, **157**
Parmesan 160, 166
    Parmesan crumbs 154, **155**
parsley
    courgette ribbon kimchi 106, **107**
    kimchi butter 183
    kimchi 'nduja pasta 166, **167**
    summer herb kimchi 101
parsnip kimchi 117
pasta
    kimchi & butter pasta with Parmesan crumbs 154, **155**
    kimchi mac & cheese 142, **143**
    kimchi 'nduja pasta 166, **167**
    kimchi pasta with gochujang butter 176, **177**
pasties, steak, Stilton & kimchi 174, **175**
patience 13
pear 22, 23, 31
    asparagus-chive kimchi 92–3
    baek kimchi 69
    beetroot & pear kimchi 109
    buchu kimchi 68
    carrot, ginger & pear kimchi 112, **113**
    dongchimi 72–3
    gaji kimchi 80–1
    geotjeori 78–9
    goguma mul kimchi 98–9
    kale & sweet potato kimchi 110–11
    kimchi-mari guksu **148**, 149
    kkaennip kimchi 82
    mak kimchi 62–3, **64–5**
    nectarine & kohlrabi white kimchi 104
    oi-sobagi 76–7
    pa kimchi 66, **67**
    pogi kimchi 59–60, **61**
    yeolmu kimchi 74–5
    see also Asian pear
pepper (bell)
    baek kimchi 69
    kimchi & quinoa one-pot stew 135
perilla leaves
    kkaennip kimchi 82
    watermelon rind kimchi 100
philosophies of kimchi 11–12
plum syrup *see* maesil-cheong
pogi kimchi 59–60, **61**
    kimchi & egg fried rice **172**, 173
pork
    bossam (boiled pork) kimchi 22
    budae jjigae (army stew) 138, **139**
    pork belly & well-fermented kimchi stir-fry 164, **165**
potato
    kimchi & potato gratin 140, **141**
    steak, Stilton & kimchi pasties 174, **175**
prawn, kimchi jeon 156–8, **157**
preparing kimchi 51–2
pumpkin
    kimchi risotto with roasted squash 160, **161**
    pumpkin & sage kimchi 114
Pyongan-do 23

quesadilla, kimchi 180, **181**
quinoa & kimchi one-pot stew 135

radish 16–17, 21, 22, 31, 33–4, 44–5
    chonggak kimchi 70–1
    yeolmu kimchi 74–5
    see also mu (Korean radish); yeolmu

radish tops 21, 23
   yeolmu kimchi 74–5
regional diversity of kimchi 17, 21–4
rice
   kimchi & egg fried rice **172**, 173
   kimchi risotto with roasted squash 160, **161**
rice drinks 29
rice porridge (juk) 33, 49
rice syrup 82, 83
rinsing and draining 13, 51–2

saeujeot (fermented shrimp) 11, 17, 22, 48
safety issues 10
sage & pumpkin kimchi 114
salt 11, 12, 16, 20, 23, 32–4, 38–42
   fine sea salt 39, 41
   food-grade rock salt 39–41
   functions 38, 42
   kosher 38–9, 41
   low-sodium 17
   measurement 41
   non-food grade salt 40, 41
   over-salty kimchi 184
   sea salt flakes 39, 41
   table salt 40, 41
   traditional (Korean solar salt/cheonil yeom) 38, 41
salting (brining) 13, 19, 30, 34–5, 41–2, 51–2
   brine-salting 51
   dry-salting 51, 71
   salting day 52
sandwich, kimchi grilled cheese 136, **137**
sauces 140, **141**, 147, 150, **151**, 156–8, **157**, 178–9
   blended kimchi 182–3
   cheese 159
   chogochujang **128**, 129
   classic blended kimchi 182
   dipping 140, **141**, 147, 150, **151**, 156–8, **157**, 178–9
   spicy, sweet kimchi glaze 183
sauerkraut 28, 32–4
sausage
   budae jjigae 138, **139**
   see also 'nduja
Savoy cabbage kimchi 115
seafood 33
   fermented *see* jeotgal
seasonal diversity of kimchi 17, 18, 22–3, 31, 54–5, 84–122
seasoning 13, 30
seaweed 23
Seo Yu-gu 16
Seoul 22, 23
serving kimchi 53–4
sesame seed 130, 132, 135, 140, 142, 150, 156–8, 162, 164, 176
shin-kimchi (sour, well-fermented kimchi) 146
shrimp (fermented) 11, 17, 22, 48
shrimp (salted) 21
   chonggak kimchi 70–1
smell of kimchi 185
soul of kimchi 13
soy sauce 13, 22, 29, 30, 31
soy-based pastes 17
spam *see* ham/spam
spinach
   kimchi & quinoa one-pot stew 135
   kimchi & spinach stuffed flatbreads 168, **169**
spring kimchi 86–94
squash
   kimchi risotto with roasted squash 160, **161**
   pumpkin & sage kimchi 114
squid 22, 48
   kimchi jeon 156–8, **157**

starter cultures 12
steak, Stilton & kimchi pasties 174, **175**
stews
   budae jjigae (army stew) 138, **139**
   kimchi & quinoa one-pot stew 135
   kimchi jjigae with mushrooms & tofu 162, **163**
stir-fries
   pork belly & well-fermented kimchi stir-fry 164, **165**
   stir-fried kimchi udon with greens 132, **133**
storing kimchi 32, 36–7
sugar 31–2
summer kimchi 96–106
summer rolls, kimchi **128**, 129
superfoods 31
swede 122
sweet potato
   kale & sweet potato kimchi 110–11
   purple sweet potato kimchi 98–9

temperature 36, 54
texture 38, 49, 60, 63, 184
thyme 109
timeline of kimchi 34–7, 185
toast
   kimchi avocado 126, **127**
   kimchi baked beans on sourdough 152, **153**
   kimchi grilled cheese sandwich 136, **137**
   kimchi tofu scramble on 130, **131**
tofu
   budae jjigae 138, **139**
   kimchi jjigae with mushrooms & tofu 162, **163**
   kimchi tofu scramble on toast 130, **131**
   vegan kimchi mandu 178–9
   vegan kimchi mandu jeongal 147
tomato
   cherry tomato kimchi 102, **103**
   kimchi baked beans on sourdough 152, **153**
tools 52–3
troubleshooting 184–5
turnip 16, 122
turnip tops, yeolmu kimchi 74–5

umami 11, 13, 21, 28, 34, 36, 47–50, 60, 70, 81, 134, 146, 160, 166, 170, 182
UNESCO, Intangible Cultural Heritage of Humanity 18

water 50
water (mul) kimchi 23, 32
   see also dongchimi
watermelon rind kimchi 100
well-fermented kimchi
   spicy, sweet kimchi glaze 183
   well-fermented kimchi risotto with roasted squash 160, **161**
white films 185
wild garlic kimchi 88–9
winter kimchi 116–22
winter root vegetable kimchi 122, **123**

yeast 29, 185
   Kahm's 32
   yeast fermentation 28, 29
yeolmu (young summer radish) kimchi 17
   recipe 74–5
Yeongdong 22
Yeongseo 22
yoghurt 180
   see also Greek yoghurt

ACKNOWLEDGEMENTS

Writing KIMCHI has been one of the most meaningful journeys of my life. This book would not exist without the love, encouragement, and support of so many people who walked beside me.

First, to my family – you are at the heart of everything I do. To my mother, Younghae Lee, thank you for every ounce of love you poured into me and for shaping who I am. Though memory fades, your warmth and spirit stay with me every day. To my sister, Jieun Kim, who has stood by me through every step of my life – I am forever grateful. To Ann and Peter, your constant love and encouragement have lifted me more than words can say. And to my husband, Matt, and our children Lily and William – you are my joy and my heart.

To my wonderful publisher, Yellow Kite, especially to Lydia, who first suggested we write a kimchi cookbook together, and to Charlotte, for bringing together such a talented and creative group. To Kimberly Espinel and Holly Cowgill – your artistry and vision brought these pages to life so beautifully. And to everyone behind this book – thank you for your care and dedication.

To my friends and mentors – Sam Cooper, Claire Ptak, Jungsik Yim, Jonny Drain, Huw Richards, Charlie Porter, Angela Chou, Nivi Jasa, Karon Ng, Izaak Adams, Spela Turk, Maria Livings, Marie Westlake, Jiyae Kim, Jungsimje, Pierre Bureau, Alan McFetridge, Stewart Walton, Sam Walton, Jimi Lee, Luis Mulet and Jiyun Lapthorn – your wisdom, inspiration, and encouragement gave me strength. And to everyone who has ever shared a jar of kimchi with me – this book is for you.

First published in Great Britain in 2026 by Yellow Kite
An imprint of Hodder & Stoughton
An Hachette UK company

1

The authorised representative in the EEA is Hachette Ireland, 8 Castlecourt Centre, Castleknock Road, Castleknock, Dublin 15, D15 YF6A, Ireland

Copyright © Jihyun Kim 2026
Photography copyright © Kimberly Espinel 2026
Author Photograph © Sam Walton
Kimchi Map of Korea Illustration by Karon Ng
Vegetable Illustrations by Angela Chou & Nivi Jasa

The right of Jihyun Kim to be identified as the Author of the Work has been asserted by her in accordance with the Copyright, Designs and Patents Act 1988.

All rights reserved. No part of this publication may be reproduced, stored in a retrieval system, or transmitted, in any form or by any means without the prior written permission of the publisher, nor be otherwise circulated in any form of binding or cover other than that in which it is published and without a similar condition being imposed on the subsequent purchaser. A CIP catalogue record for this title is available from the British Library

Hardback ISBN: 9781399755283
eBook ISBN: 9781399755290

Publishing Director: Lydia Good
Senior Project Editor: Charlotte Macdonald
Designer: Ami Smithson
Photography: Kimberly Espinel
Food Stylist: Holly Cowgill

Colour origination by Alta Image London
Printed and bound in Dubai by Oriental Press Dubai

Hodder & Stoughton policy is to use papers that are natural, renewable and recyclable products and made from wood grown in sustainable forests. The logging and manufacturing processes are expected to conform to the environmental regulations of the country of origin.

Yellow Kite
Hodder & Stoughton Ltd
Carmelite House
50 Victoria Embankment
London
EC4Y 0DZ

www.yellowkitebooks.co.uk
www.hodder.co.uk